WILD FLOWERS AT A GLANCE

WILD FLOWERS
AT A GLANCE

by

M. C. CAREY

and

DOROTHY FITCHEW

*Illustrated throughout
in full colour*

LONDON
J. M. DENT AND SONS LTD

J. M. DENT & SONS LTD.
Aldine House · Bedford St. · London

Made in Great Britain
by
The Temple Press · Letchworth · Herts
First published 1949

CONTENTS

PREFACE

AT A GLANCE

IN the year 1817 Messrs. Longman, Hurst, Rees, Orme & Brown published a book called *Conversations on Botany*. It is illustrated by exquisite engravings in delicate colour, and contains much information imparted in the manner of the time.

Edward, a small boy, holds eighteen instructive conversations with his mother, in which she methodically answers his questions.

'What are you doing, Mamma?'
'I am examining the pretty little yellow flower that we found this morning in the hedge.'

They then go on to discuss botany in general, its use (about which Edward seems not a little dubious), and the parts of a flower. This is their first 'conversation.'

With the remark that 'an indolent person can never expect to become a good botanist,' Edward's mother gives her son a list of twenty-four botanical classes to learn (from *Monandria* to *Crypto-gamia*). Edward wilts slightly at this, but Mamma goes on unmoved to the list of orders (*Monogynia* to *Siliquosa*), kindly adding that 'it is not necessary for you to learn at present the orders of the five remaining classes, which are also difficult.'

At last Edward goes for his first 'walk in the fields.' He finds a Germander Speedwell. But he does not discover the name of this 'nice little blue flower,' until Mamma has lectured him on it for some time,. and decided that it is in the class *Diandria* and of the order *Monogynia*.

When she has got to the end of the eighteenth talk (on seaweeds and fungi) Mamma stops.

'I have now told you, my dear Edward,' she says, 'all that I intended to mention about botany. I shall be very much gratified if your desire to pursue it is at all increased by anything I have said.'

Now *Wild Flowers at a Glance* is not at all the kind of book that Mamma would have chosen for Edward. She would despise the easy way. Yet we find the French philosopher, Ernest Bersot, writing: 'To be learned is too lofty an ambition for the greater number of us.' And he was actually discussing the question of the illustration of plants and flowers printed as a direct help in finding out their names.

The translation of the passage runs:

To the ignorant these books with illustrations are precious. If it is only a drawing it is well; if it is a coloured one it is better still. How much trouble it saves us! Suppose we were obliged to seek through a number of rooms for an unknown person, how difficult, even if aided by the most minute description, it would be to recognize him, and how easy to stumble upon someone else! If, on the contrary, he himself or his portrait is shown to us, in a glance, without analysing any details, an image of his general appearance is formed in our minds by which we can always recognize him.

In a word, then, what is the real matter in question? *Recognition.* . . .

Based, then, on this idea, that most of us are not very learned and know very little botany, this note-book has been compiled, and is a collection of over 260 'portraits' of British wild flowers, few of those included being rare.

The brief notes are very elementary. The main grouping is non-botanical for the flowers are arranged in (normal) colour sections.

Eager flower-lovers and beginners will, we hope, from this simple start of mere recognition soon go on to the fascinating and more serious study of our wild flowers. They will equally soon, we also hope, discover that it is not necessary for their enjoyment to pick all the specimens they find. On another page is given a list of valuable and useful books to which searchers may turn, ranging from hand-books with simple botanical notes to scientific *Floras*.

But to return for a moment to Edward—we, too, would be gratified if any one using this little book should find their interest in wild flowers 'increased,' as well as his 'desire to pursue botany' for its own sake.

M. C. C.

NOTE

As there are over 1,200 British wild flowers and only 264 can be illustrated in the present volume, it is obvious that there are very many gaps. The flowers have all been found by the artist or compiler, and each drawing made immediately from the specimen.

Many authorities have been freely consulted, particularly Bentham and Hooker's *Handbook of the British Flora* (seventh edition). Only a seasonal indication as to time of flowering is given, as the vagaries of our climate are so great, and these dates are in line with the above *Flora*.

Reference has already been made to the non-botanical arrangement of the flowers into five colour groups. Within these the *genera* or families are in the sequence adopted by Bentham and Hooker, and the individual *species* or flowers follow the same authorities in the order in which they set within their families.

A six-inch rule is printed on the back cover of the book for easy field measurement.

Grateful thanks are due to Mr. A. J. Wilmott, of the British and European Herbaria of the British Museum, who has been unfailingly kind and patient in identifying every specimen and authoritatively pronouncing upon it. His nomenclature has been adopted throughout.

Mr. Charles Lee has meticulously checked, and in a number of cases supplied, derivations from the Greek and Latin for the flower names, and has thus provided a valuable contribution to the notes.

SOME HELPFUL BOOKS

Handbook of the British Flora. G. Bentham and J. D. Hooker. Seventh edition revised by A. B. Rendle. (Reeve.)

Illustrations to Bentham and Hooker's *Handbook of the British Flora*. Seventh edition. Fitch and Smith. (Reeve.)

Everyman's Wild Flowers and Trees. Miles Hadfield. (Dent.)

Wild Flowers of the Wayside and Woodland. T. H. Scott and W. J. Stokoe, based upon *Wayside and Woodland Blossoms* by Edward Step. (Warne.)

A Flower Book for the Pocket. Macgregor Skene. (Oxford University Press.)

Common Wild Flowers and *More Common Wild Flowers*. 2 vols. John Hutchinson. (Pelican Books.)

BOTANICAL WORDS USED IN THIS BOOK

Bract. Small leaves growing closely under the flower, when very small often called *scales*. Or they may be small leaves at the axil of the flower stalk.

Calyx. The ring of sepals that encloses the petals of a flower.

Carpel. One of the divisions of the ovary or seed vessel.

Involucre. A ring of bracts or bract-like leaves that surrounds a flower or a cluster of flowers.

Node. The place on the stem from which the leaf springs.

Petals. The inner leaves, usually coloured, that form the corolla of a flower.

Sepals. The outside part of a flower, usually a ring of small greenish leaves, but sometimes the same colour as the petals. They protect the bud.

Stamens. The male part of the flower that produces *pollen* in its tiny heads or *anthers*.

Stipules. Small leaves that grow in pairs at the foot of the leaf stalk or leaf. When the real leaves are small the stipules protect them.

Style. The little stalk in the centre of a flower which is part of the *pistil*, running from the ovary or seed vessel (the female part of a flower) to the *stigma* at its tip. It is on the *stigma* that the *pollen* has to fall for fertilization and the formation of seeds to take place.

Viscid. Sticky.

Vittae. Tiny oil tubes found in the fruits of the *Umbelliferae* (the Carrot family), which are visible as stripes on the outside of the fruit.

1

WHITE FLOWERS

TRAVELLER'S JOY or OLD MAN'S BEARD
Clematis Vitalba

Found: Hedges, thickets, chalky districts.   Common in southern England.
Flowers: Summer.   *Height:* Climbs and trails to great lengths.

The flower has no real petals, but four, sometimes five, thick greenish-white sepals curl back so that the central mass of pale yellow stamens stands out.   The flowers grow in bunches at the end of short stalks and have a pleasant scent.   The styles grow out into plumy tails so that in the autumn the hedge over which the plant climbs seems covered with a feathery cloud.

The leaves are usually cut into five egg-shaped pointed leaflets, the leaf stalks twisting and twining like tendrils to support the plant.

The main stem is woody and may grow very thick and shrub-like. It is hard and ribbed, with swollen ridged joints, and is tinged with red; it may grow many yards long.

Clematis: From Gk. *klēma*, 'tendril or vine twig.'
Vitalba: From Lat. *vitis*, 'vine,' and *alba*, 'white.'

2

G Sand ~~EEE~~ 1832

Cognitive analytical
therapy

CAT (Sian Ph.)

WOOD ANEMONE or WINDFLOWER

Anemone nemorosa

Found: Woods and copses.   Common in Britain.   *Flowers:* Early spring.
Height: 4–9 in.

These delicate white flowers (1–1½ in. across) are often tinged with pink, more deeply so on the underside, and grow singly at the head of slender stalks.

Two-thirds up the stalk grow three deeply cleft fern-like leaves, stalked and softly hairy underneath.   The root leaves grow upright some way from the flower stalks, and are larger and broader, deeply divided into three toothed parts.

The stem is hairy and tinged with a dull red.   The leaf stems are more slender than those of the flowers.

Anemone: From Gk. *anemos*, 'wind,' as the plant flowers in a windy season.
Nemorosa: Lat., 'of the woods.'

3

LARGE WHITE WATER-LILY
Nymphaea alba

Found: Lakes, ponds, slow rivers.   Fairly common in Britain.   *Flowers:*
Summer.   *Height:* Flower lies on surface of water.

The plants root in the mud, and send long stalks to the surface of
the water, where the large white scentless flowers (about 3–4 in. across)
and most of the leaves float.

The leaves are smooth and heart-shaped, almost circular, and thick
and leathery with plain edges.

The stalks are long and have fine air-canals running through them
to give them buoyancy and provide the plant with air.

Nymphaea: The Latinized Greek name.   Water-lilies were dedicated to
the nymphs by the Greeks.

Alba: Lat., 'white.'

4

SLENDER-FRUITED WATERCRESS
Nasturtium uniseriatum

Found: Wet places, ditches, streams.   Common in Britain.   *Flowers:* All the summer.   *Height:* 6 in.–2 ft.

Small four-petalled flowers grow in clusters at the ends of the stems or branches.   The pods are very slender and curve upwards, the seeds in one row.

The leaves are cut into pairs of oval leaflets, the end leaflet larger than the others, smooth, and very slightly toothed.

The hollow stem is branched, floats in water, creeps on mud, or rises from wet places.

Nasturtium: Lat. for a kind of cress, from *nasus,* 'nose,' and *torquere,* 'to twist,' the pungent taste being apt to cause one to wrinkle one's nose.

Uniseriatum: From Lat. *unus,* 'one,' and *series,* 'a row.'

5

JACK-BY-THE-HEDGE

Sisymbrium Alliaria

Found: Borders of lanes, fields, and hedgerows.   Common in Britain, but less so in northern and western Scotland.   *Flowers:* Spring.   *Height:* 1–3 ft.

Sometimes called *Garlic Mustard*.

A tall upright plant.   The small flowers, each with four crosswise petals, are soon succeeded by little stiff spine-shaped pods, about 2 in. long, which tend to curve upwards.   The plant smells of garlic when bruised, especially the stem.

The leaves appear first in early spring.   They vary in shape and may be heart-shaped and roundly toothed, or almost triangular with pointed teeth.   They are smooth above and hairy underneath.

The stem is strong, sparsely hairy above, thickly covered with white hairs below.

Sisymbrium: The Latinized Gk name of a species of cress.

Alliaria: From Lat. *allium*, 'garlic.'

6

COMMON
SCURVY-GRASS
Cochlearia officinalis

Found: Marshes, seashores, muddy waste land, and sometimes on mountain rocks. Common in Scotland, fairly so in England and Ireland. *Flowers:* All the summer. *Height:* Up to 8–10 in.

Small four-petalled flowers, sometimes tinged with purple (about ⅓ in. across), grow in clusters at the head of the angular, smooth, fleshy stem, and are scented.

The root leaves grow on long stalks and are usually round or kidney-shaped, while the stem leaves are stalkless and clasp the stem with projecting ears, and have a few broad teeth or lobes.

The seed pods are round.

Cochlearia: From Lat. *cochlear,* 'spoon,' see shape of lower leaves.
Officinalis: From Lat. *officina,* 'workshop,' because the plant was used by the old herbalists.

7

DANISH SCURVY-GRASS
Cochlearia danica

Found: Sandy and muddy foreshores. Common in England, less so ın
Scotland and Ireland. *Flowers:* Summer. *Height:* 3–9 in.

Compare with the other *Scurvy-Grasses* (pp. 7 and 9) and note that
the leaves are different, stalked and shaped somewhat like ivy leaves.
The flowers are bunched at the head of the rather fleshy stem. The
rounded pods narrow at each end.

Cochlearia: From Lat. *cochlear,* 'spoon,' see shape of lower leaves.
Danica: Lat., 'Danish.'

8

ENGLISH SCURVY-GRASS

Cochlearia anglica

Found: Marshes, seashores, muddy waste land. Fairly common in England and Scotland, rare in Ireland. *Flowers:* All the summer. *Height:* 12–18 in.

The plant is often taller and the flowers are larger than the *Common Scurvy-Grass* (p. 8). It grows is wet places near the sea or estuaries, often amongst grass, and in a very variable plant in different parts of the country. The illustration is of the Hampshire form.

The slender smooth stem ends in a spray of small white sweetly scented flowers, each of four petals; they grow on short stalks and turn into small pods.

The leaves in Hampshire are narrow and pointed, the upper ones are arrow-shaped, the lower ones simpler, sometimes shorter and broader.

Cochlearia: From Lat. *cochlear*, 'spoon.'

Anglica: Lat., 'English '

9

SHEPHERD'S PURSE

Capsella Bursa-pastoris

Found: Waste ground, banks, and roadsides. Very common in Britain.
Flowers: Nearly all the year round. *Height:* 6in.–1 ft. Varies much.

A common weed. The little flowers grow in a long spike on the upper part of the stem, and as they wither the heart-shaped seed pods form, until there is a loose open spike of pods below the last-opened cluster of flowers at the top.

The leaves are arrow-shaped with toothed edges, and clasp the stem, while those from the root lie in a rosette on the ground, and may be deeply cut or notched, or very much less so.

The slender stem is upright, branched, and often hairy.

Capsella: Lat., 'a little box.'

Bursa-pastoris: Lat., 'the purse of the shepherd.' (*Bursa* is a medieval Latin word taken from a Greek word meaning 'skin' or 'hide.')

HOARY CRESS
Lepidium Draba

Found: Waste places. Fairly common, especially in Kent. *Flowers:* Spring and early summer. *Height:* About 1 ft.

A downy plant. The little white flowers grow in short spikes that spread out to give a rather flat appearance. They form into little pods.

The upper leaves clasp the stem; ear-shaped and pointed at their bases. The lower leaves are stalked.

The stem is stout and upright, branching above.

Lepidium: From Gk. *lepidion*, diminutive of *lepis*, 'a scale, because the little pods are like scales.

Draba: Gk., 'mustard.'

11

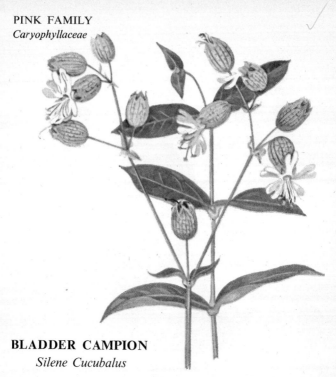

BLADDER CAMPION

Silene Cucubalus

Found: Waste ground, banks, edges of cornfields.   Spread over Britain.
Flowers: All the summer.   *Height:* 6 in.–1 ft.

The five white petals are deeply notched, and the stamens and mauve styles stick out beyond them.   The flowers grow in loose clusters, each with a curious calyx—a $\frac{1}{2}$-in.-long mauvish-green bladder, veined with dark lines, and cut at the top into fine teeth.   When the petals wither the rounded bladder remains.

The leaves are stalkless, soft to the touch, smooth, though fringed with tiny hairs; they clasp the stem and grow in pairs, tapering to a point.   They have a soft 'bloom' on them, and plain edges.

The stem is much branched, erect, the flowering stalks springing from the leaf axils.   The stem is swollen at these joints like most of the stems of the Pink family, and breaks off easily there.

Silene: From Lat. *Silenus*, the satyr.
Cucubalus: Lat. name of a medicinal plant mentioned by Pliny.

WHITE CAMPION

Melandrium album

Found: Banks, hedges, and cornfields. Common in Britain. *Flowers:* Summer. *Height:* 1–2 ft.

Very like the *Red Campion* (p. 199) with its five deeply cut petals, the flowers growing in loose clusters. They are slightly scented at dusk and tend to open at night, attracting moths. The calyx is ribbed and rather swollen, has five teeth, and is covered with soft hairs.

The leaves and stem are hairy, and the latter is sticky at the joints. The leaves grow in pairs with smooth edges, the upper clasp the stem, the lower are stalked and taper at their bases.

Melandrium: Lat., 'honey flower,' or possibly named after an Italian botanist, Melandri.

Album: Lat., 'white.'

13

THREE-VEINED SANDWORT
Arenaria trinervia

Found: Shady and damp places, ditches. Common in England and Ireland, less so in Scotland. *Flowers:* Spring and summer. *Height:* A few inches to a foot.

Compare with the *Chickweed* (p. 16) which this *Sandwort* much resembles, but the petals are rounded and not cut; they are shorter than the very pointed sepals.

The leaves, which are about ½ in. long, have three very marked veins or nerves, from which the plant gets its name.

The slender flower stalks spring from the axil of the leaves and the main stem, which is branched, lies on the ground, or spreads upwards.

Arenaria: Lat., 'pertaining to sand,' on which so many of the plants are found.
Trinervia: Lat., 'three-nerved.'

COMMON MOUSE-EAR CHICKWEED
Cerastium vulgatum

Found: Fields and waste places, cultivated ground. Common throughout Britain. *Flowers:* Spring and summer. *Height:* 6 in. or more.

The flowers grow in clusters at the head of the stem, the white petals deeply notched, and generally slightly longer than the sepals. A common weed.

The leaves grow in pairs on the stem and are stalkless, but have stalks when growing from the root, the upper leaves are shaped like a mouse's ear. They are covered with soft hairs and the whole plant is downy. It forms matted tufts later in the season.

The stem is branched from the base and varies much in height, from a few inches to quite a tall plant. It is covered with sticky hairs.

Cerastium: From Gk. *kerastion*, diminutive of *keras*, 'a horn,' because of the shape of the capsules.
Vulgatum: Lat., 'common.'

15

CHICKWEED

Stellaria media

Found: Waste places, roadsides, cultivated ground, sandy seashores. Common throughout Britain. *Flowers:* All the year round. *Height:* A few inches, lies along the ground.

A common weed. The tiny white petals of the flower are shorter than the green sepals enclosing them, and are deeply cut.

The leaves are stalked below, but clasp the stem above. A line of white hairs runs up one side of the stem which is weak and straggling and inclined to spread along the ground.

Stellaria: From Lat. *stella*, 'a star.'
Media: Lat. 'middle' or 'medium' size.

16

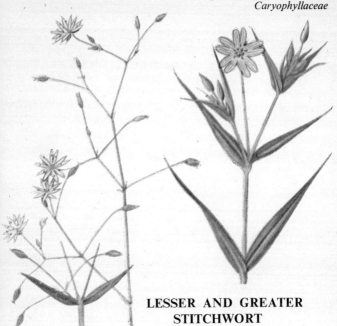

LESSER AND GREATER STITCHWORT

Stellaria graminea and Stellaria Holostea

Lesser Stitchwort
Found: In fields and hedgerows.   Common in Britain.   *Flowers:* All the summer.   *Height:* 1–2 ft.

Greater Stitchwort
Found: Hedgerows, bushy places, open woods.   Common in Britain
Flowers: Spring and early summer.   *Height:* 1–2 ft.

These two Stitchworts with their gleaming star-like flowers are rather alike, but the difference can be clearly seen in the drawings.

The *Lesser Stitchwort* is more straggling and grass-like in leaf and stem, and has smaller flowers that grow on widely branched stems. The petals of each are cleft, those of the *Greater Stitchwort* being much longer than the sepals.   Both have square stems.

Both plants tend to grow in masses, the stems so slender and brittle that they lean against grass and other plants.

Stellaria: From Lat. *stella*, 'a star.'   *Graminea:* Lat., 'grass-like.'
Holostea: From Gk. *holos*, 'whole,' and *osteon*, 'bone.'

17

CORN SPURREY

Spergula arvensis

Found: A cornfield weed. Common in Britain. *Flowers:* Summer.
Height: 6 in.–1 ft.

A slender branching little plant; the minute flowers grow in forked
clusters, the stalks turning down as the flowers fade.

The leaves are needle-shaped and grow in two clusters spaced
together up the stem, but actually look as if they grew in rings.

The stem is straggling, branched from the base and downy.

Spergula: From Lat. *spargere*, 'to scatter,' because of the many seeds, or
because in some fields it grows densely.

Arvensis: Lat., 'of the fields.'

18

PERFOLIATE CLAYTONIA

Claytonia perfoliata

Found: Copses and heaths. Common in England. *Flowers:* Spring and summer. *Height:* 4 in.–1 ft.

A curious little plant that is really North American, but now a common weed in this country.

The small bunches or spikes of white or whitish-green little flowers grow at the head of a round soft stem in a ring inside the leaves, which are united to form a single rounded leaf like a cup. The stem passes through the centre of the leaf, as it were, which is rather like a half-open umbrella, turned upside-down.

The lower root leaves are flat and spade-like in shape, with the same plain edges as the upper leaves.

The stalks spring from the root and are pale pink; they lie on the ground or stand erect. The whole plant is fleshy, and very smooth.

Claytonia: Named in memory of John Clayton, an early American botanist.

Perfoliata: From Lat. *per*, 'through,' and *foliatus*, 'leaved,' meaning 'through the leaf,' a feature of the stem as described above.

19

WOOD SORREL
Oxalis Acetosella

Found: Woods, shady damp places. Common in Britain. *Flowers:* Early spring. *Height:* 4–6 in.

Delicate little plants that carpet the woods, especially those that are damp and covered with leaf-mould. The five petals are veined with pink or lilac (about ½ in. long) and grow singly at the head of fragile stalks.

The leaves are very thin and a clear bright green, cut into three heart-shaped leaflets. These tend to bend backwards close to the stem, each leaflet backing on to the others so tightly that if eased apart they at once close up backwards again. They are covered with fine white hairs and sometimes have a purplish tinge underneath.

The stems are very fragile and tinged with pink. They all spring from the creeping root. The flower stalks are longer than the leaf stems, and half-way up have a pair of tiny bracts.

The plant is very poisonous to cattle.

Oxalis: From Gk. *oxus,* 'sharp,' because the leaves have a sour taste.
Acetosella: Lat. diminutive of *acetosus,* 'sour,' from *acetum,* 'vinegar.'

DUTCH CLOVER

Trifolium repens

Found: Meadows and fields. Common in Britain. *Flowers:* The whole summer. *Height:* 6 in.–1 ft.

The flowers grow in rounded heads on long stalks, and are white, sometimes tinged with pink. When the flower heads fade, each little pea-shaped flower droops as the seed sets inside small pods, and turns brown. The flowers are sweetly scented and full of honey.

The trefoil leaves have a faint white crescent mark, and are finely toothed.

The stems are smooth, and creep and root.

Trifolium: Lat., 'three-leaved.'
Repens: Lat., 'creeping.'

B

21

MEADOW-SWEET

Ulmaria hexapetala

Found: Damp places, water meadows. Common in Britain. *Flowers:* Summer. *Height:* 2–3 ft.

Compare with *Dropwort* (p. 23).

Sweet - scented flowers with a strong woody stem tinged with red. The dense flower spikes have a fluffy effect. The leaves are cut into five to nine oval leaflets, often 2–3 in. long, toothed, downy, and white underneath, the end leaflet three - lobed. There are pairs of minute leaflets between the larger ones, and ear-shaped stipules.

Ulmaria: Lat., 'elm-like.'
Hexapetala: Gk., 'having six petals.'

DROPWORT

Spiraea Filipendula

Found: Downs, dry fields, chalky places. Frequently found in England and Scotland, and in a few places in the west of Ireland. *Flowers:* Summer. *Height:* 1–2 ft.

Very like *Meadow-sweet* (p. 22) but has no scent, and is a much smaller plant altogether, though with larger flowers. These grow in spikes and the buds are pinkish, opening out into creamy white petals.

The leaves grow chiefly from the root, and are about 3 to 5 in. long, very much cut into toothed segments, which are slightly downy. They are of a deep green.

The stem is strong, woody, and reddish in colour.

Spiraea: From Gk. *speira*, 'coil,' referring to the fruits, which are spirally coiled.

Filipendula: Lat., 'hanging by a thread.'

23

WILD STRAWBERRY
Fragaria vesca

Found: Shady places, clearings in woodlands. Common in Britain.
Flowers: Early summer. *Height:* Creeping.

Compare with the *Barren Strawberry* (p. 25), especially as regards the leaves, which are so much more strongly veined and grooved, larger and more oblong, and covered with silky hairs. Long slender runners root to form new plants, leaving the rootstock, from which also several stalked leaves spring, as well as the straight stem that bears the branched clusters of flowers. These subsequently become the well-known small scarlet or creamy yellow berries.

Fragaria: From Lat. *fragum,* 'strawberry.'
Vesca: Lat., 'little.'

BARREN STRAWBERRY
Potentilla sterilis

Found: Dry banks, sheltered open spaces in woodlands. Common in England, Ireland, and southern Scotland. *Flowers:* Early spring. *Height:* Creeping.

Very like the *Wild Strawberry* (p. 24) but bears no ripening berry as fruit and has no runners; the flowers are usually smaller.

The plant branches from the root and has a tufted appearance, with silky root leaves and hairy stalks. The leaves are not so grooved as those of the *Wild Strawberry*; they are divided into three-toothed leaflets.

Potentilla: Lat., 'powerful,' because of its supposed medicinal qualities.
Sterilis: Lat. 'non-fruitful.'

FIELD ROSE
Rosa arvensis

Found: Hedges and thickets. Common in England and Ireland, less so in Scotland. *Flowers:* Summer. *Height:* Trails to great lengths.

Very like the *Dog Rose* (p. 217) but scentless, and white, with much longer trails. The flowers are 2 in. across, in clusters, and the plant grows in long arching trails, with hooked prickles.

The leaves are smooth and shiny, the leaf stalks winged at their bases, with a reddish midrib.

The stem is tough, woody, and a deep red.

Rosa: The Latin name, from Gk. *rhodon*, 'rose.'
Arvensis: Lat., 'of the fields.'

THREE-FINGERED SAXIFRAGE
Saxifraga tridactylites

Found: Stony places, on walls and rocks.   Not uncommon in England and Ireland and eastern Scotland.   *Flowers:* Spring and early summer.   *Height:* 2–5 in.

Tiny five-petalled flowers grow singly from very slender reddish stalks, only ⅙ in. across and tending to droop.   The five lobes of the calyx are nearly as long as the petals.

The leaves are very small and wedge-shaped springing mostly from the root in a little rosette; the stem leaves are stalkless, hairy, either oblong and plain-edged, or with three small finger-shaped lobes.

The stem is covered with sticky hairs, reddish, and rises erect, generally branching.

Saxifraga: From Lat. *saxum,* 'rock,' and *frangere,* 'to break.'

Tridactylites: From Gk. *tri-,* 'three,' and *daktulos,* 'finger,' i.e. 'having three fingers.'

27

SANICLE

Sanicula europaea

Found: Borders of woods, thickets, shaded lanes. Fairly common in Britain. *Flowers:* Summer. *Height:* 1–1½ ft.

The clusters of flower heads are usually three only, each on short stalks branched from the head of the stem. A longer stem grows out from the main stalk lower down, also usually with three little branched heads. The stamens are conspicuous, as the outer ring of tiny flowers in each head is made up only of stamens with no petals. The fruits turn into little burs, covered with barbed prickles, which helps to distinguish this plant from others in the same family.

The leaves grow mostly from the root on long stalks, 1–2 in. across; they are deeply cut into five broad lobes, which are cut again and toothed.

The stem is smooth and leafless, with narrow bracts at the axil of the flower stalks.

Sanicula: From Lat. *sanare*, 'to heal,' because of the supposed healing qualities of the plant.
Europaea: 'Of Europe,' where the flower grows.

GOUTWEED
Aegopodium Podagraria

Found: Waste places, often near buildings, in damp woods. Common in Britain. *Flowers:* Summer. *Height:* 18 in.–2 ft.

Also called *Bishopweed* or *Herb Gerard.*

A garden weed, and spreads quickly with creeping roots, the Goutweed is a coarse plant that grows in masses, made up of fairly closely spaced flower clusters, each on separate short stalks. Each tiny flower has five petals, the tips turned up, and deeply notched.

The root leaves are roughly triangular and grow on long stalks, cut into three quite distinct oval parts, which are again cut into three, 2 to 3 in. long and sharply toothed. The stem leaves are few and much smaller: narrow leaflets sheathed at their base.

The stem is erect, hollow, furrowed, and branched.

The fruits are oval and flattened, ridged, with the styles closely bent back.

Aegopodium: From Gk. *aix*, 'goat,' and *pous*, 'foot.'

Podagraria: From Gk. *podagra*, 'gout.' The old herbalist, Culpeper, says of the plant: 'the very bearing of it about one easeth the pains of the gout.'

COMMON BURNET SAXIFRAGE
Pimpinella Saxifraga

Found: Fields, roadsides, dry places. Common in Britain.
Flowers: All the summer.
Height: 1–2 ft.

Do not confuse with the Saxifrage family.

Umbrella-like clusters of flat flower heads, usually ten to fifteen, radiate loosely on slender 'spokes.' The seed pods are oval and smooth, with two stigmas curving outwards.

The leaves vary very much, and are so cut as to form pairs of leaflets deeply notched or lobed. The upper narrow leaves are smaller and more delicately cut into deeply toothed narrow pairs, so much so that they have almost a fringed look.

The stem is tall and erect, furrowed, and downy near the top.

Pimpinella: From the medieval *pipinella*, which comes from *bipinnula*, 'two - winged,' bipinnate, referring to the leaves.
Saxifraga: From Lat. *saxum*, 'rock,' and *frangere*, 'to break.'

HEMLOCK WATER-DROPWORT
Oenanthe crocata

Found: Ditches, wet places, banks or streams. Common in Britain.
Flowers: Summer. *Height:* 2–5 ft.

Dense clusters of flower heads, on stalks 2 in. or more long, grow at the head of the stem. The fruits have been described as 'corky,' and are narrow, with broad ribs and upright hard styles.

The leaves are broad and wedge-shaped, deeply cut twice or three times.

The stem is stout and grooved, and much branched.

This is a very poisonous plant and the roots, which form tubers rather like narrow carrots, have been known to prove fatal when mistaken for that vegetable. The juice of the stem and roots turns yellow when exposed to the air. Never feed the leaves or roots to animals.

Oenanthe: From Gk. *oinos*, 'wine,' and *anthos*, 'flower,' because the flowers have a slight scent of wine.

Crocata: Lat., 'saffron-yellow,' in allusion to the colour of the juice.

31

CARROT FAMILY
Umbelliferae

FOOL'S PARSLEY
Aethusa Cynapium

Found: Fields and roadsides, banks and hedgerows.   Common in England and Ireland but not in northern Scotland.   *Flowers:* Summer and early autumn.   *Height:* 1–2 ft.

These umbrella-like heads are a little smaller than some others of this family, and may be distinguished by the three long thin strips (bracts) at the base of each little flower cluster, but with no bracts from the general flower head.

The leaves are finely cut and give a lacy effect to the plant as it grows in masses.

The stem is smooth, hollow, branched, and marked with lines.

The plant is generally smooth, and has rather an unpleasant smell with a bitter poisonous taste, very unlike that of the real garden parsley.

Aethusa: From Gk. *aithō,* 'I burn,' because of the plant's acrid taste.
Cynapium: From Gk. *kuon,* 'dog,' and Lat. *apium,* 'parsley,' a hybrid word, emphasizing the fact that the plant has none of the good qualities of the real parsley.

COW PARSNIP or HOGWEED
Heracleum Sphondylium

Found: Fields, woods, and hedgerows. Common in Britain. *Flowers:* Summer and autumn. *Height:* 4–6 ft.

A tall coarse plant which can grow to a great height, with leaves a foot long. The plant is hairy and rough all over, and has an unpleasant pigsty smell. The large umbrella-shaped heads of flowers are usually white, but can be tinged with pink.

The leaves have loose enveloping sheathes forming their base and clasping the stem. They are deeply cut into separate large broad lobes, cut again, and toothed.

The stem is thick, hollow, and hairy, much grooved, and stands dead and brown all through the winter.

The fruits are globular in shape with conspicuous vittas (oil tubes) between ridges, but these only go half-way down.

Heracleum: From Herakles, Gk. name for Hercules, possibly because of the robust nature of the plant.
Sphondylium: Gk. name for 'cow parsnip.'

ROUGH CHERVIL

Chaerophyllum temulum

Found: Hedgerows, banks, and waysides. Common in England, less so in Ireland and the Scottish Highlands. *Flowers:* Summer. *Height:* 2–3 ft.

The flower clusters grow on loosely and widely spaced short umbrella-like stems, the points of the petals bent inwards.

The leaves are fern-like and downy, with large coarse teeth, deeply cut into wedge-shaped lobes.

The stem is hollow, furrowed, hairy below and smooth above. When the plant grows large and coarse it has a reddish tinge, especially at the joints, and is covered with white hairs.

The fruits are about $\frac{1}{3}$ in. long, smooth, and without ribs.

Chaerophyllum: From Gk. name of the plant, *chairephullon.*
Temulum: Lat., 'drunken' or 'causing vertigo.'

WILD CARROT

Daucus Carota

Found: Fields, roadsides, and waste places near the sea.   Common throughout Britain.   *Flowers:* Summer and autumn.   *Height:* 1–3 ft.

The broad heads of the numerous flower clusters are slightly hollowed like saucers, and gradually close over like cups.   The tiny inner flowers have a pinkish tinge, and note the minute red flower in the centre of the head.   There is a collar of small leaflets (bracts) round the main flowering head like small forked spines.

The leaf stalks are flattened out to clasp the stem, and the leaves are finely divided and fern-like.

The stem is solid, tough, ridged, and hairy.   It is indeed a hairy plant all over.

The fruit is oval and covered with prickles.

Daucus: From Gk. *daukon*, 'a plant of the parsnip or carrot kind.'
Carota: Lat., name for 'carrot.'

35

HEMLOCK

Conium maculatum

Found: Waste places, banks of streams. Not particularly common, but may be found all over Britain. *Flowers:* Summer. *Height:* 3–5 ft.

About twelve clusters of tiny flowers grow at the head of the stem on branched stalks. Three short bracts grow below each cluster, all drooping to one side, and bracts also droop from the base of the general flower head. (Compare with *Fool's Parsley*, p. 32.)

The leaves are large and fern-like, giving the plant a very leafy appearance. The stem is furrowed, distinctively spotted with purple, and much branched. The fruits are flat on their inner sides, rounded on the outer, with prominent wavy ridges. The plant has an unpleasant mousy smell and is poisonous.

Conium: From Gk. *konos*, 'cone,' referring to shape of the fruits.
Maculatum: Lat., 'spotted.'

36

HEDGE BEDSTRAW
Galium Mollugo

Found: Grassy banks, thickets, fields. Common in England and southern Scotland; rare in Ireland. *Flowers:* Summer. *Height:* 1–3 ft., or more in hedges.

A straggling plant. The flowers, in dense masses, cluster at the end of branched stems.

The leaves grow in rings, usually six to eight, egg-shaped or narrowly pointed, with rough edges and tiny pointed tips.

The stem is weak, smooth, shining, and branched.

Galium: From Gk. *gala,* 'milk,' because some plants of this group were used to curdle milk for cheese-making. If eaten by cows when the plant is in full flower, their milk will tend to go sour quickly.

Mollugo: From Lat. *mollis,* 'soft,' i.e. lacking hooks or burs.

37

CLEAVERS
Galium Aparine

Found: Hedges, bushy places. Common in Britain. *Flowers:* Summer. *Height:* Several feet.

Sometimes called *Goose-grass*. Dense masses grow at the foot of hedgerows, clinging with tiny hooks that cover the stem, leaves, and fruit. The flowers grow in loose clusters on opposite stalks springing from the leaf axils.

Four to ten leaves grow in rings, narrow and pointed, and often over an inch long. The stem is square, trailing and spreading, and covered with tiny hooks.

The small fruits. covered with hooked bristles, form burs, and stick closely to everything with which they come in contact. But occasionally they are smooth.

Galium: From Gk. *gala,* 'milk,' because some plants of this group were used to curdle milk for cheese-making.

Aparine: Gk. name of the plant.

WOODRUFF
Asperula odorata

Found: Woods and copses, especially beech woods.   Common in Britain.
Flowers: Spring and early summer.   *Height:* 6 in.–1 ft.

The small flowers grow in loose branched clusters at the head of the stem, and have a scent of hay when picked and slightly dry.   They are funnel-shaped and turn into small fruits with hooked bristles.

The leaves, as the name implies, look like green ruffs up the stem. They grow in regular rings of seven to nine, and are smooth, narrow, and pointed.   They are slightly rough at the edges.

The stem is slender, upright, smooth, and square.

Asperula: Lat., 'rather rough,' referring to the leaves
Odorata: Lat., 'sweet-smelling.'

DAISY

Bellis perennis

Found: Waysides, fields, lawns.　Common throughout Britain.　*Flowers:*
Nearly all the year round.　*Height:* a few inches.

The commonest British wild flower, and needs little description.
The flowers grow at the end of short stalks from the centre of a
rosette of spoon-shaped leaves that usually grow tightly pressed to the
ground.　The flowers tend to close at night.

The leaves grow from the root and are slightly toothed.

Bellis: Lat., 'pretty.'

Perennis: From Lat. *per*, 'through,' and *annus*, 'year,' i.e. 'living the
year through, or perpetual.'

40

OX-EYE DAISY

Chrysanthemum Leucanthemum

Found: Meadows and fields. Common throughout Britain. *Flowers:* Late spring and summer. *Height:* 1–2 ft.

Sometimes called the *Dog Daisy*, this large (1½–2 in. across) brilliantly white flower grows in masses in hayfields and pastures, but varies much in size. The flower is cupped in overlapping layers of little scales with brown and purple edges. The centre is a bright yellow.

The leaves from the root have long stems and are coarsely toothed, while the stem leaves are stalkless and only slightly toothed.

The stalk is strong, furrowed, and slightly branched.

Chrysanthemum: From Gk. *chrusos*, 'gold,' and *anthemon,* 'flower.' The generic name really belongs to *C. segetum,* the *Corn Marigold* (see p. 120), a 'golden flower.'

Leucanthemum: From Gk. *leukos*, 'white,' and *anthemon,* 'flower.'

FEVERFEW

Chrysanthemum Parthenium

Found: Waste places, roadsides, a garden escape. Fairly common in Britain but not in Ireland. *Flowers:* Summer. *Height:* 1–2 ft.

The small daisy-like flowers grow in loose bunches at the head of the main stem, each flower on its own stalk (about ⅜ in. across). The plant has a strong aromatic scent.

The leaves are downy, broad, much divided and notched.

The stem is upright and branched.

Chrysanthemum: From Gk. *chrusos,* 'gold,' and *anthemon,* 'flower.' (See note, p. 41.)

Parthenium: Gk., 'virginal,' in allusion to the pure white flowers.

SCENTLESS MAYWEED
Matricaria inodora

Found: Waste ground, fields.   Common in Britain.   *Flowers:* Throughout summer and autumn.   *Height:* 12–18 in.

Very like the *Wild Chamomile* (p. 44), but with larger flowers (1–1½ in. across), and yellow centres which are not so conical.   The flowers grow at the head of long smooth stalks, and have very little scent.   The involucral bracts are edged with brown.

The leaves are so much cut as to be almost threadlike, and have no stalks; they grow alternately up the stem, tending to give the plant a rather bushy appearance.

The stem is smooth, much branched, and spreading.

Matricaria: From Lat. *matrix*, 'womb,' because the plant was thought to be good for uterine diseases.

Inodora: Lat., 'without scent.'

43

WILD CHAMOMILE

Matricaria Chamomilla

Found: Fields and waste places. Throughout Britain. *Flowers:* All through the summer. *Height:* 8–18 in.

This plant is very like the *Scentless Mayweed* (p. 43), but its daisy-like flowers ($\frac{1}{2}$–$\frac{3}{4}$ in. across) are slightly smaller and it has a strong, sweet, aromatic scent. The white petals are short and blunt; the flowers grow at the end of slender branched stalks, with rounded yellow centres, pushed up like thimbles as the petals fade. The involucral bracts do not have brown edges like those of the *Scentless Mayweed*.

The leaves are so cut up as to be almost thread-like. The stem is erect and branching.

Matricaria: From Lat. *matrix*, 'womb,' because the plant was thought to be good for uterine diseases.
Chamomilla: From Gk. *chamai*, 'on the ground,' and *mēlon*, 'apple.'

STINKING MAYWEED

Anthemis Cotula

Found: Waste and cultivated places. Common in southern England and Ireland, less so in the north and rare in Scotland. *Flowers:* All the summer and autumn. *Height:* 1 ft. or more.

A common weed. The daisy-like flowers grow at the head of slender stalks in very loose, widely spaced clusters. The plant may be smooth or hairy, but it is not downy. It gives off a very unpleasant strong smell when rubbed (compare with the sweet aromatic scent of the *Wild Chamomile* (*Matricaria Chamomilla*) (p. 44).

The leaves are very narrowly divided, almost as if fringed, the upper ones less so than the lower. They are smooth and covered with tiny glands which contain the bitter ill-smelling juice.

The stem is slender and branched.

Anthemis: From Gk. *anthos*, 'a flower.'
Cotula: Lat., 'a small vessel.'

45

SNEEZEWORT
Achillea Ptarmica

Found: Hilly places, commons, and moist fields.   Common in Britain.
Flowers: Rather late summer.   *Height:* 1–2 ft.

This plant has a greyish look, and is covered with whitish hairs.
At first its little daisy-like flowers (¾ in. across) have a pale greenish-grey centre, which later turns yellow.   The square-ended petals, about
eight to twelve, are notched.

The leaves are long and narrow and taper to a point; they are
covered with fine hairs and have almost imperceptible teeth.

The stem is erect, stiff and hard, and is branched near the top.

Achillea: Named after Achilles, who is supposed to have been the first to
discover the healing virtues of the plant.

Ptarmica: From Gk. *ptarmikos*, 'causing to sneeze,' because the powdered
leaves were once used as snuff.

YARROW
Achillea Millefolium

Found: Waste ground, fields, and roadsides. Very common in Britain.
Flowers: The whole summer. *Height:* 1 ft.

Sometimes called *Milfoil*. The crowded heads of small white flowers are often tinged with pink (p. 227). They grow together at the top of the branched stems in flat heads, unlike most other flowers in this family.

The leaves are so cut and divided as to give the plant a feathery appearance, and they mostly spring from the root.

The stem is strong and upright, a greenish-grey colour and ridged, and covered with soft woolly hairs.

The plant is usually very hairy, but can be found quite smooth.

Achillea: Named after Achilles, who is supposed to have been the first to discover the healing virtues of the plant.

Millefolium: Lat., 'bearing a thousand leaves.'

47

GREATER BINDWEED

Convolvulus sepium

Found: Hedgerows and thickets.   Common in England and Ireland, local in Scotland.   *Flowers:* Summer.   *Height:* Twines and trails to 6–7-ft. lengths.

Large pure white flowers, trumpet-shaped, grow singly, each flower stalk springing from the leaf axil.

The plant is sometimes called *Hooded Bindweed*, for a green hood —two heart-shaped bracts—encloses the calyx, which is hidden underneath.

The leaves are large, smooth, and pointed, arrow-shaped and angular at the base, or egg-shaped.

The stem twines round any support it can find.

Convolvulus: From Lat. *convolvere,* 'to twine.'

Sepium: Lat., 'of the hedges.'

COMFREY
Symphytum officinale

Found: Ditches, shady and wet places. Fairly common in England and Ireland, less so in Scotland. *Flowers:* Spring and summer. *Height:* 2–3 ft.

Usually a rather coarse, tall, heavy plant, covered with hairy bristles. The flowers are bell-shaped, yellowish-white, or pink (p. 243). They droop in one-sided spikes, each flower pinched in at the end as if by a finger-nail.

The leaves are large, coarse, bristly, and aromatic. They may be nearly a foot long. The lower leaves are stalked, those from the stem run down it, giving it a winged appearance.

The stem is thick, soft, deeply grooved, and very hairy.

Symphytum: From Gk. *sumphuein,* 'to unite,' because the plant was formerly thought helpful in healing wounds.

Officinalis: From Lat. *officina,* 'workshop,' because the plant was used by the old herbalists.

49

BLACK NIGHTSHADE

Solanum nigrum

Found: Waste places, sea beaches. Common in southern England.
Flowers: Summer and autumn.   *Height:* About 1 to 2 ft.

A common garden weed.   The bright yellow stamens are conspicuous as they stick out from the petals, which tend to curve backwards.   The plant is smooth.

The leaves are stalked, egg-shaped, and the edges waved with a few broad teeth.

The stem is much branched.

The fruit is green at first, turning black, but occasionally yellow or red.

Solanum: Lat. name for the plant.
Nigrum: Lat., 'black.'

WHITE DEAD-NETTLE
Lamium album

Found: Under hedges, grassy roadsides, waste places. Almost all over Britain. *Flowers:* Spring, until the end of the year. *Height:* Varies from 6 to 7 in. to 1 ft. or more.

Creamy-white velvety flowers grow in rings of eight to ten, where the leaves join the stem. Compare with the *Red Dead-nettle* (p. 262), for both have a tube and high arched downy hood, fringed with soft hairs, over an open mouth and cleft protruding lip. The buds are like round furry balls. The plant usually grows in masses.

The leaves are hairy, toothed and stalked, and often tinged with red. The stalk is square and also tinged with red.

Lamium: Lat. for 'dead-nettle,' from the same Gk. stem as *lamia,* 'a monster,' referring to the odd appearance of the flower.

Album: Lat., 'white.'

51

LARGE WHITE HELLEBORINE
Cephalanthera Damasonium

Found: Chalky places, woods. Chiefly southern England. *Flowers:* Early summer. *Height:* 12–18 in.

Creamy-white flowers stand upright in loose spikes at the top of the stem, the effect rather leafy as the green bracts below each flower look like narrow leaves, the lower ones longer than the flower. The petals are joined together almost up to their tips, and curve over the round yellow lip, which is divided in two.

The leaves clasp the stem, grow from 1 to 3 in. long, and are ribbed and lance-shaped.

There are no root leaves.

The ovaries below each flower are slightly twisted.

Cephalanthera: From Gk. *kephalē*, 'head,' and *anthēra*, 'anther' from the shape of the anther.
Damasonium: A plant name used by the Roman, Pliny.

52

SNOWDROP
Galanthus nivalis

Found: Woods and shady places.   *Locally common in Britain.   *Flowers:*
Early spring.   *Height:* 4–6 in. or even 1 ft.

The *Snowdrop* is not really a native of this country, but it is now
found growing wild in many places.

The buds are like drops of snow, and they open into drooping three-
cornered flowers, the inner petals being edged and lined with delicate
green, while the three outer sepals are a pure white.

The leaves are long, narrow, and smooth, the edges tending to bend
or keel inwards.   They go on growing after the flowers have withered.

The stem is straight and unbranched, with a long bract enclosing
the bud.

Galanthus: From Gk. *gala*, 'milk,' and *anthos*, 'flower.'
Nivalis: Lat., 'belonging to snow,' referring to the time of flowering—very
early spring—or to the flower's colour; or to both.

FRITILLARY
Fritillaria Meleagris

Found: Damp fields and meadows, rather rare. Truly wild only in southern and eastern England; not in Scotland or Ireland. *Flowers:* Spring. *Height:* 12–18 in.

Compare with the chequered variety of this lovely bell-shaped flower (p. 270) which droops singly at the head of the stem.

The flower head is made up of six floral leaves, which are oblong or narrowly oval, narrowing to a point, and about 1½ in. long. The flower opens out into a wide bell with bright yellow stamens in the centre.

The leaves are narrow and grass-like, 6–8 in. long, and grow from the stem.

The stem is slender and upright, leafy, with a slightly reddish tinge.

Fritillaria: From Lat. *fritillus,* 'dice-box,' in allusion to the chequered board on which dice were thrown, as these flowers are more usually chequered in colour.

Meleagris: Gk., 'guinea-fowl,' referring to the usual markings of the flower, like that bird's feathers.

COMMON STAR OF BETHLEHEM

Ornithogalum umbellatum

Found: Wood and fields. Fairly frequently found in England. *Flowers:* Spring and early summer. *Height:* 4 in.–1 ft.

Star-like six-petalled flowers (1–1½ in. across) grow at the head of an upright stem in a cluster of about six to ten flowers; it is more a cluster than a spike, as the lower flower stalks lengthen so as to bring the flowers almost on a level with each other. A green line runs up the back of each petal.

The leaves are long and narrow and spring from the bulb, with a white line down their centre, and bending or keeling inwards.

The stem is upright and leafless, with withered-looking bracts at the angle of each flower stalk.

Ornithogalum: From Gk. *ornis,* 'bird,' and *gala,* 'milk,' i.e. 'bird's milk,' in other words, a marvel.

Umbellatum: From Lat. *umbella,* 'sunshade,' i.e. 'with flowers growing umbrella-fashion.'

55

RAMSONS or
BEAR'S GARLIC
Allium ursinum

Found: Woods, damp shady places. All over Britain. *Flowers:* Spring and early summer. *Height:* 6–8 in.

This plant often grows in masses, covering a slope or part of a wood. It has a strong smell of garlic and a bulb like an onion. The starlike flowers grow in a loose cluster of about twelve flowers at the head of the long stalk.

Two membranous bracts completely enclose what appears to be a single flower bud. Then they split apart and the whole cluster of flowers spreads out.

The long leaves remind one of those of the *Lily-of-the-Valley*, and sheathe the foot of the main flower stem. They are lance-shaped, thin and flat, smooth, and very soft, about 6–8 in. long.

The stem is three-sided.

Allium: Lat., 'garlic.'
Ursinum: Lat., 'pertaining to a bear.'

2

GREENISH-WHITE,
GREEN,
or
GREENISH-YELLOW
FLOWERS

SETTERWORT

Helleborus foetidus

Found: Chalky stony places. Not common, but found in southern and eastern England. *Flowers:* Early spring. *Height:* 1 ft. and over.

Sometimes called the *Stinking Hellebore*. A curious plant which is very poisonous and has an unpleasant smell.

The flowers grow in loose clusters and hang down; the pale green sepals, tipped often with purple, enclose the flower-like goblets. The little tube-like petals are shorter than the many stamens.

The upper leaves clasp the stem. The lower leaves are much divided, stiff, shining, and toothed, forming a thick tuft.

The stem is upright.

Helleborus: The Greek name for the plant.
Foetidus: Lat., 'evil-smelling.'

WHITE BRYONY
Bryonia dioica

Found: Hedges, woods, and thickets. Fairly common in England, rare in the north and in Wales, not found in Scotland or Ireland. *Flowers:* Summer. *Height:* Trails several feet long.

Do not confuse with *Black Bryony* (*Tamus communis*) which also climbs, but has shining heart-shaped leaves and belongs to a different family.

The plant climbs to great lengths by means of tendrils coiled like springs. It is covered with hairs. The flower has five petals, greenish-white veined with a darker green. Male and female flowers grow on different plants. Straggling withered stems festoon the hedges in autumn with orange or red berries.

The leaves are stalked, shaped rather like vine leaves, deeply divided into five to seven toothed lobes, the centre one longer than the others and pointed. They are hairy and often 5–7 in. across.

The stem is rough, hairy, and branching, supported by the spirally twining tendrils.

Bryonia: Lat. name of the plant, from Gk. *bruein*, 'to swell, burst forth.'
Dioica: From Gk. *di-*, 'two,' and *oikos*, 'house,' i.e. having staminate and pistillate flowers on different plants.

IVY

Hedera Helix

Found: On trees, old walls.   Common in Britain.   *Flowers:* Late autumn.
Height: Climbs to great heights.

An evergreen climber that can grow to such a thickness of trunk that it is almost like a tree itself though supported by one.   Yellowish-green flowers grow in clusters, turning later into black or yellow berries.

The leaves are leathery and shining, usually five-pointed, but they vary greatly and the leaves of flowering shoots are quite simple and lance-shaped.

The branches that bear flowers are bushy.   The main stem climbs and the lower slender branches spread along the ground.   Small root-like suckers cling to anything up which the ivy is climbing.

Hedera: Lat. name for the plant.
Helix: Gk. name for a kind of ivy (='spiral').

60

MUGWORT
Artemisia vulgaris

Found: Waste places and roadsides. Common in Britain. *Flowers:* End of summer and autumn. *Height:* 2–3 ft.

A rankly growing shrubby plant that tends to grow in masses, with small flowers bunched up the stalk in woolly spikes. The flowers are reddish-yellow, bell-shaped, and hang down.

The leaves grow thickly, alternately up the stem, and are cut into sharply pointed lobes and then cut again. They are smoothly downy above and very white and silvery underneath, covered with white hairs.

The stem is red, ribbed, stiff and straight, rough and rather woody, branched above.

The plant has an aromatic smell.

Artemisia: From Artemis, the Greek goddess, whom the Romans identified with their Diana.
Vulgaris: Lat., 'common.'

TOOTHWORT
Lathraea Squamaria

Found: On the roots of trees, specially hazel, and in shady places. Not uncommon in England and Ireland, and the southern counties of Scotland. *Flowers:* Early spring. *Height:* 6–16 in.

A whitish, flesh - coloured plant tinged with blue or red. This is a parasite which grows on the roots of trees, especially hazel.

The flowers hang in close spikes, mostly on one side of the stem, and are about $\frac{1}{2}$ in. long. The purplish petals lie inside the calyx, which is two-lipped and pale; there are four stamens and a long style that hangs down.

There are no leaves, but the stem is fleshy and thick, the rootstock being covered with thick, short, fleshy scales, set closely together.

Lathraea: From Gk. *lathraios*, 'hidden' or 'secret,' because of the shady and rather hidden places where this plant is found.

Squamaria: Lat., 'furnished with scales.'

GREATER PLANTAIN
Plantago major

Found: Waste places, roadsides, dry fields. Very common in Britain.
Flowers: Summer and autumn.   *Height:* 4–12 in.

A common weed of the garden, with long slender flower spikes of brownish-green. The whitish stamens and the purple anthers stick out and give the spike a feathery look.   The seeds are black and hard.

The leaves are egg-shaped, broad, and strongly ribbed; all spring from the root with strong foot stalks.

The flower stems are strong and round, and grow tough with age.

Plantago: From Lat. *planta*, 'sole of the foot,' because the leaves lie close to the ground.

Major: Lat. 'greater.'

63

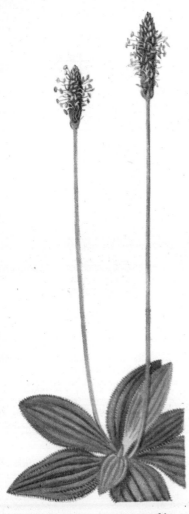

LAMB'S-TONGUE PLANTAIN
Plantago media

Found: Roadsides, rough fields, waste places, pastures on calcareous soils. Common in England and southern Scotland but not in Ireland. *Flowers:* Early summer and Autumn. *Height:* 8–18 in.

Sometimes called the *Hoary Plantain* because of the pink silvery effect of the flower heads, which are shorter than the *Greater Plantain* (p. 63) and more slender than the *Ribwort Plaintain* (p. 65). The spike is about 2 in. long, with the tiny flowers growing round the club-like head. The mauve stamens are conspicuous. After flowering the spike becomes hard and brown with seeds.

The leaves lie close to the ground in a rosette, preventing grass from growing underneath. They are short and broad, and have usually five prominent ribs. They are velvety to the touch and covered with short, white downy hairs.

The stem is hairy, very upright, and leafless.

Plantago: From Lat. *planta*, 'sole of the foot,' because the leaves lie close to the ground.
Media: Lat., 'middle' or 'medium' size.

64

RIBWORT PLANTAIN
Plantago lanceolata

Found: Fields, waste places. Common in Britain. *Flowers:* The whole season. *Height:* 6–18 in.

The most common of the plantains, distinguished by its narrow leaves, which can grow very tall in long grass. The club-like head is about 1–2 in. long, or can be smaller; the tiny flowers grow round it, and the long white stamens hang out, giving the head a fringed, feathery look. When the seeds form the head becomes hard, brown, and rough.

The leaves grow from the root and are narrow, tapering, and lance-shaped, with three to five prominent ribs on their undersides. They are slightly hairy, with very slightly toothed edges. There are no stem leaves.

The stem is very erect, slender, and square.

Plantago: From Lat. *planta,* 'sole of the foot,' because the leaves lie close to the ground.

Lanceolata: Lat., 'like a spear-head,' because of the shape of the leaves of this plantain.

BROAD-LEAVED DOCK
Rumex obtusifolius

Found: Waste places, roadsides, fields. Common in Britain. *Flowers:*
Summer and early autumn. *Height:* 2–3 ft.

The small flowers grow thickly up the stem in rings, and are tinged
with red.

The lower leaves are oval, stalked, large and broadly rounded at
the base, sometimes 8–9 in. long, with dark red midribs. The upper
leaves are much smaller, narrower, and lance-shaped.

The stem is stout, ribbed, and erect.

Rumex: Lat., 'sorrel.'

Obtusifolius: Lat., 'having blunt or rounded leaves.'

DOG'S MERCURY
Mercurialis perennis

Found: Woods, shady places.   Common in England and Scotland.   Less so in Ireland.   *Flowers:* Early spring.   *Height:* 6–15 in.

A common woodland plant, this plant grows in masses in the undergrowth.

The tiny greenish-yellow flowers have no real petals, only sepals, and there are male and female flowers.   The former grow in spikes on long stalks, springing from the leaf axils, and are much yellower than the female flowers because of their conspicuous stamens.   The female flowers grow two or three together in shorter spikes and are greener. The two kinds of flowers grow on separate plants.

The fruit is green, two round seed pods are joined together and covered with minute hairs.

The leaves are mostly bunched together on the upper part of the stem, pointed, toothed, hairy, about 2–4 in. long.   There are minute stipules at the base of the leaf stalk.

The stem is erect, hairy, and unbranched.

Mercurialis: After the god Mercury, who was said to have discovered the healing qualities of the plant.

Perennis: Lat. *per*, 'through,' and *annus*, 'year,' i.e. living the year through, or perpetual.

67

ANNUAL MERCURY

Mercurialis annua

Found: Gardens, waste places, cultivated fields. Common in England and Ireland. Local in Scotland. *Flowers:* Summer and autumn. *Height:* 6–12 in.

Compare with *Dog's Mercury* (p. 67) and note that this plant has smooth shiny leaves, and not hairy ones. It also flowers later in the season. The male and female flowers usually grow on different plants, the former in slender spikes, the latter only two or three together.

The leaves are stalked and grow opposite each other; they are shiny and thin with coarse teeth. The stem is upright and smooth.

Mercurialis: After the god Mercury, who was said to have discovered the healing qualities of the plant.
Annua: Lat., 'annual'—springing up, flowering, seeding, and dying within a year.

STINGING-NETTLE

Urtica dioica

Found: Waste places and cultivated ground.   Common in Britain.   *Flowers:*
Summer and autumn.   *Height:* 2–3 ft.

The well-known weed.   The flowers grow in drooping tassels, and
the plant is usually to be found in dense masses.   It is covered with
down and stinging bristly hairs.   The male and female flowers are
usually on separate plants.

The leaves grow in pairs, are broadly lance-shaped, regularly toothed,
the lower ones broader than the upper, with short stems.

The stem is strong and upright.

Urtica: From Lat. *urere*, 'to burn,' on account of the stinging hairs.

Dioica: From Gk. *di-*, 'two,' and *oikos*, 'house,' i.e. having staminate and
pistillate flowers on different plants.

CUCKOO-PINT or LORDS-AND-LADIES
Arum maculatum

Found: Woods, thickets, shady places. Fairly common in England and Ireland. *Flowers:* Early spring. *Height:* 6 in.–1 ft.

The pale green hood (bract leaf) tapers to a point and is almost transparent. In the centre, carefully protected, is a deep purplish, club - shaped spike, smooth and tall. The base of the hood folds over itself like an envelope to protect the real flower hidden below the spike, with a fringed ring of white stamens. Later the seeds can be seen below this again, and they turn in the autumn into scarlet poisonous berries which cluster at the head of a short stem after the hood and the rest of the flower have withered away.

The large leaves are shiny, dark green, arrow-shaped, often spotted with purple. They have strongly marked veins and come up well before the flower stalk, usually in March.

Arum: Lat. form of the Gk. name of the plant, *aron.*

Maculatum: Lat., 'spotted,' referring to the leaves.

TWAYBLADE

Listera ovata

Found: Damp places, woods, fields, chalky
hills. Fairly common in Britain. *Flowers:*
Spring and summer. *Height:* 1–1½ ft.

This orchis has a very distinctive pair
of leaves, but is otherwise rather like the
Man Orchis.

The greenish-yellow flowers grow in
long open spikes, each with a short stalk,
and a long hanging divided lip; the sepals
are greenish and the petals more yellow.

There are usually only two broad
egg-shaped leaves, which grow opposite
each other about
4–6 in. up the
stem. They are
smooth, with
plain edges, and
2–4 in. long.

The stem is up-
right, rounded,
and very downy.
It has some
sheathing scales
at the foot.

Listera: After Dr. Martin Lister, a British
naturalist.
Ovata: From Lat. *ovum,* 'an egg,' in allusion
to the shape of the leaves.

71

HERB PARIS

Paris quadrifolia

Found: Damp fields and woods and calcareous soil.   Not very common in Britain.   *Flowers:* Spring and early summer.   *Height:* 9 in.–1 ft.

Curious flowers (1½ in. across) with yellowish-green lance-shaped sepals, and almost thread-narrow yellowish petals. A blue-black berry develops from the ovary.

The leaves are mostly four in number and grow in a ring, from which the single flower stem rises. They are smooth, oval, and pointed at each end; about 3–4 in. long.

The stem is rounded.

Paris: Either from Lat., *par,* 'equal,' referring to the leaves, or from the name of the Trojan prince.

Quadrifolia: Lat. 'four-leaved.'

3

YELLOW FLOWERS

LESSER CELANDINE
Ranunculus Ficaria

Found: Waste ground, roadsides, fields, woods, and banks. Very common throughout Britain, except in the West Highlands of Scotland. *Flowers:* One of the earliest spring flowers to appear. *Height:* Up to 6 in.

Brilliantly burnished star-like flowers, tinged with green on the undersides of the eight or nine pointed petals. The flowers grow singly on stalks as long as the leaves. They tend to close in cold dull weather and open in the sun. The plant grows in masses. The smaller leaves are ivy-shaped. Those from the root grow on long stems and are smooth and shining, heart-shaped or broadly triangular with wavy edges; sometimes they have whitish patches or brown blotches.

The stem is slender and soft and sometimes tends to creep.

Ranunculus: From Lat. *rana,* 'frog,' because most plants of this family like damp places.

Ficaria: Lat., 'fig-like,' on account of the root tubers.

74

GOLDILOCKS
Ranunculus auricomus

Found: Woods, shady, and damp places. Fairly common in England, less so in Ireland and Scotland, and rare in the Highlands. *Flowers:* Spring. *Height:* Up to 1 ft.

Sometimes called *Wood Crowfoot*.

Compare with the *Buttercup* (p. 77), but it is easily distinguished because the five petals are usually of different sizes, and the flower often looks as if it were deformed and imperfect. It is also a smoother plant.

The leaves are very diverse. The upper ones are stalkless, and divided right down to the main stem into narrow and pointed smooth strips, with plain edges. The root leaves have long stalks and are rounded, and divided into three-toothed broad lobes.

The stem is upright, round, and slightly branched.

Ranunculus: From the Lat. *rana*, 'frog,' because most of the plants of this family like damp places.

Auricomus: Lat., 'golden-haired,' from *aurum*, 'gold,' and *coma*, 'hair of the head.'

UPRIGHT MEADOW CROWFOOT

Ranunculus acer

Found: Meadows and fields, waste places, and cultivated ground. Very common in Britain. *Flowers:* Throughout the summer. *Height:* 1–3 ft.

The many different kinds of Buttercups are rather alike except in detail.

This is one of the tallest, though varies a great deal, and is covered with soft hairs. The flowers are rather large and open out till they are almost flat. The sepals do not bend back on the stalk as they do in the *Bulbous Buttercup* (*R. bulbosus*).

The leaves are deeply cut and are stalked, with wedge-shaped segments which are cut again. The upper leaves are cut more simply, and are narrower.

The stem is upright and branched, and note that the flower stalk is *not* furrowed, and is round.

Ranunculus: From Lat. *rana,* 'frog,' because most plants of this family like damp places.

Acer: Lat., 'sharp,' referring to the bitter poisonous juice of the plant.

BUTTERCUP
Ranunculus repens

Found: Almost everywhere.　*Flowers:* All the summer.　*Height:* 6 in.–1 ft.

This is the original Buttercup of old botanists, though a number of flowers in the family are called Buttercups, which vary only slightly from each other.

This one has the burnished golden petals forming a cup-like shape associated with all Buttercups, and the flowers grow on an upright plant.　Look for its runners which shoot out from the root, rooting themselves at every node (where the leaf joins the stem) and forming new plants.　The plant is seldom as high as a foot.

The leaves are divided into three stalked distinct parts, each one much cut and toothed, and the centre one longer than the other two, so that the whole leaf taken together has an oval, pointed shape.

The stem grows sideways, and is short and stout, giving off runners. The flower stalk is furrowed.

Cattle avoid buttercups because of their poisonous and bitter juices.

Ranunculus: From Lat. *rana*, 'frog,' because most plants of this family like damp places.
Repens: Lat., 'creeping.'

SMALL-FLOWERED CROWFOOT

Ranunculus parviflorus

Found: Waste places, dry banks. Not particularly common in England and Ireland and not found north of Durham. *Flowers:* Spring and summer. *Height:* 4 in.–1 ft.

A spreading hairy plant lying on the ground, with little flowers only ¼ in. across or less, each with three to five petals.

The nutlets are covered with hooked prickles.

The leaves are almost round, with blunt curved teeth; the lower leaves usually cut deeply into five lobes.

The flower stems are short, slender, and weak, and rise only a few inches.

Ranunculus: From Lat. *rana,* 'frog,' because most plants of this family like damp places.

Parviflorus: 'Having small flowers,' from Lat. *parvus,* 'small,' and *flos* 'flower.'

CORN CROWFOOT

Ranunculus arvensis

Found: Cornfields. Common in southern England, decreasing north-wards and rare in Ireland. *Flowers:* Summer. *Height:* 6 in.–2 ft.

A common weed of the cornfields with small flowers like miniature buttercups, of a pale yellow, and only ½ in. across. The nutlets are covered with hooked spines, a distinguishing point about this plant.

The leaves are very deeply cut into narrow segments.

The stem is erect and a pale green, slightly hairy, and not furrowed.

Ranunculus: From Lat. *rana,* 'frog,' because most plants of this family like damp places.

Arvensis: Lat., 'of the fields.'

79

MARSH MARIGOLD or KING-CUP

Caltha palustris

Found: Water meadows, marshy places, and ditches.   Common in Britain.
Flowers: Throughout the spring and early summer.   *Height:* About 1 ft.

Large, widely cup-shaped flowers, the petals like burnished gold, with a central tuft of golden stamens.

The leaves grow chiefly from the root on long stout stalks, and are broad and shining, heart-shaped and rounded, with crinkled edges. The stem leaves have short stalks, almost stalkless near the top. There is a membrane at the axil of the leaf and the stem.

The stalks either stand erect or lie along the damp ground.   They are smooth, hollow and fleshy, and slightly grooved.

The plant tends to grow in tufts.

Caltha: Lat. name for marigold.

Palustris: From Lat. *palus,* 'marsh.'

YELLOW WATER-LILY or BRANDY-BOTTLE
Nuphar lutea

Found: Quiet water, ponds.   Common in Britain except northern Scotland
Flowers: Summer.   *Height:* Floats or rises just above the surface of the
water.

The flowers are about 2 in. across, the yellow sepals being five or
six in number and globular, enclosing a large number of petals which
are much smaller.   There are several rows of stamens.   The flowers
have a faint scent.

The leaves are usually 6–8 in. across and are heart-shaped, or almost
round, leathery and waxy, and float on the water.

The stalks are long and rise to the surface, thick and fleshy.

Nuphar: Lat. from Arabic *nufar,* 'water-lily.'
Lutea: Lat., 'yellow.'

81

GREATER CELANDINE
Chelidonium majus

Found: Hedgerows and waste ground, shady places, roadsides, near houses·
Common in England and parts of Ireland, less so in Scotland.   *Flowers:*
All the summer.   *Height:* 1–2½ ft.

Do not confuse this flower with the *Lesser Celandine* (p. 74) which
belongs to an altogether different family.

Flowers, four-petalled and loose-looking, grow in open clusters at
the head of a tall stem, each flower on its own stalk, later developing
into narrow seed pods (1½–2 in. long).

The leaves are thin and deeply divided; they are rather like oak
leaves in shape, and are a bluish green underneath.   There are white
hairs at the leaf axil.   The plant is tall and has a leafy look.

The stem is erect, branching, and full of a poisonous yellow juice.

Chelidonium: From Gk. *chelidōn*, 'a swallow,' because as an old writer
says: 'It beginneth to spring and flower at the coming of the swallow,
and withereth at their return.'

Majus: Lat., 'larger.'

YELLOW HORNED POPPY
Glaucium flavum

Found: Seashores and sandy places. Common in England and Ireland, but only in southern Scotland. *Flowers:* Summer. *Height:* 2 ft.

Shining yellow flowers, which can be 3–4 in. across. The four petals are delicately waved like goffered frills. The buds are enclosed in green cases covered with bristles, long and pointed.

The leaves are a soft blue-green, with a 'bloom' on them, like so many plants of the seashore. They are thick and leathery and clasp the stem, with hairs up the back of the mid-rib. They are deeply cut and curl in attractive shapes.

The stem is stout and spreading, much branched and very smooth.

Glaucium: From Gk. *glaukos*, 'bluish-green,' from the bloom on the leaves.
Flavum: Lat., 'yellow.'

CHARLOCK

Brassica sinapistrum

Found: Cultivated ground.   Very common in Britain.   *Flowers:* All the summer.   *Height:* 1–3 ft.

Sometimes called *Wild Mustard*.

The flowers grow at the head of the stem in a loose spike, and are about ½ in. across.   Each petal has a tiny stalk with tall stamens in the centre of the flower, which give an airy fly-away look to the heads. The flowers wither into needle-shaped seed pods with long beaks and full of black seeds, each pod about ½–1½ in. long.

The leaves are rough, large and oblong, notched and toothed.

The stem is slightly furrowed, rather hairy, and may be tinged with red.   It is erect and branched.

Brassica: Lat., 'cabbage.'

Sinapistrum: From Lat. *sinapis*, 'mustard.'

84

HEDGE MUSTARD

Sisymbrium officinale

Found: Waste ground, at the foot of walls, rubbish heaps. Common in Britain, though less so in the north of Scotland. *Flowers:* Summer. *Height:* 1–2 ft.

A very upright plant, with a wiry look. The flowers are very small ($\frac{1}{10}$ in. across), growing up the branched stems and turning into narrow little pods pressed close to the stem.

The root leaves are large, hairy, and deeply jagged into three-cornered lobes. The stem leaves are small and hairy, long, narrow, and pointed.

The stem is very erect and stiff, tough, round, and wiry. It branches out alternately and horizontally, a distinctive feature of the plant.

Sisymbrium: The Latinized Gk. name of a species of cress.

Officinale: From Lat. *officina*, 'workshop,' because the plant was used by the old herbalists.

YELLOW ROCKET

Barbarea vulgaris

Found: Damp waste places, riversides. Common in Britain. *Flowers:* Spring and summer. *Height:* 1–2 ft.

Small flowers grow in spikes, turning into dense narrow pods which stand erect or spread and curve upwards.

The leaves are deeply and narrowly cut, with a larger end leaflet. The stem leaves are small and variable.

The stem is stiff, smooth, and angular.

Barbarea: Named after St. Barbara.

Vulgaris: Lat., 'common.'

86

WILD MIGNONETTE
Reseda lutea

Found: Waste places and chalky districts. In south-east England, western and northern Ireland, and east of Scotland. *Flowers:* Summer. *Height:* About 1 ft.

Very like the garden variety but scentless. The flowers grow in stiff spikes each on a little stalk, usually with six petals. They are a greenish-yellow colour, irregularly divided.

The leaves vary, but are always very deeply cut into narrow irregular strips with waved edges.

The stem is hard and tough, thick and green, and usually curved at the base.

Reseda: From Lat. *resedare*, 'to appease or quieten,' because the plant was once used as a sedative.

Lutea: Lat., 'yellow.'

ROCK ROSE
Helianthemum Chamaecistus

Found: Dry fields, chalk downs, gravel banks. Common in England and eastern Scotland. Uncommon in Cornwall and western Scotland, and unknown in Ireland. *Flowers:* All the summer. *Height:* Low, with flowering stems a few inches to 1 ft.

A shrubby plant, with branches that lie on the ground. The flowers grow in loose spikes and open broadly with five petals ($\frac{3}{4}$–$1\frac{1}{4}$ in. across) which are soft and silky. The stamens are bunched in the centre. The sepals are five, but two are very small, and the other three have distinctive ribs. The flowers tend to droop, especially the buds.

The leaves are small and grow in pairs, and have stipules (leaflets) at their bases. The edges of the leaves are even, and they are slightly hairy above and covered with white down underneath.

The main stem is short and woody and reddish, much branched, and throws up the flowering branches, otherwise lies on the ground.

Helianthemum: 'Sunflower,' from Gk. *hēlios,* 'sun,' and *anthemon,* 'flower.'
Chamaecistus: From Gk. *chamai,* 'on the ground,' and *kistos,* 'rock rose.'

FIELD PANSY
Viola arvensis

Found: Cultivated fields and waste places.   Common in Britain.   *Flowers:*
Spring to autumn.   *Height:* 3 in.–1 ft.

Sometimes called *Field Heartsease*.

Pale yellow flowers, almost white, with a deep orange centre.   The
sepals are longer than the petals and stick out between them.   The
small flowers are just over $\frac{1}{2}$ in. across.

The leaves vary in shape from almost round to narrowly oval and
toothed.   Narrow lance-shaped or much cut little leaves (stipules)
grow at the leaf axils, so toothed as to have an almost fringed look.
These stipules, together with the leaves, sometimes give the plant a
bushy, tufted effect.

The flower stems are slender and soft, the main stem stouter.

Viola: Lat. name for 'violet.'
Arvensis: Lat., 'belonging to the fields.'

TUTSAN
Hypericum Androsaemum

Found: Open woods and thickets. The west side of Britain, Ireland, and southern England, but rare in eastern counties. *Flowers:* Summer. *Height:* 1½–2 ft.

Compare with *Common St. John's Wort* (p. 91).

There are not many flowers (¾ in. across) in the flat-shaped cluster at the head of the stem; the five petals grow closely together at their base but spread apart, and the green sepals show between them, two small and three larger. The stamens are conspicuous, and are in five bunches slightly joined at the base. The fruit is a black berry. This is a shrubby plant.

The leaves are smooth, stalkless, and grow in pairs, egg-shaped and broad, with blunt ends and rather heart-shaped at the base.

The stem is short, woody and erect, and tinged with red.

Hypericum: From Gk. *hupo*, 'under,' and *ereikē*, 'heath,' referring to the prostrate growth of some members of this group.
Androsaemum: From Gk. *androsaimon*, 'man's blood,' so called because of its blood-red sap.

COMMON ST. JOHN'S WORT
Hypericum perforatum

Found: Hedges, woods, dry copses. Common in Britain. *Flowers:* Summer and autumn. *Height:* 1–2 ft.

Compare with *Tutsan* (p. 90) of the same family. The flowers (½ in. across) grow at the head of short branched stems and make a handsome head of blossom. Each flower has five pointed petals. The stamens grow in three bunches, slightly joined at the base.

The leaves are stalkless and small, marked with transparent dots, from which the plant gets its specific name.

The stem is erect and branching at the top, very smooth and rather slender though inclined to be woody, and is ridged.

Hypericum: From Gk. *hupo*, 'under,' and *ereikē*, 'heath,' referring to the prostrate growth of some members of the group.
Perforatum: Lat., 'pierced through,' because of the transparent dots on the leaves.

FURZE or GORSE

Ulex europaeus

Found: Cliffs, dry open commons, moors, stony wastes. Common in England and Ireland and southern Scotland. *Flowers:* Spring and summer, but intermittently throughout the year. *Height:* 2–3 ft. or more.

A shrub with sharply thorned short branches, each ending in a strong thorn. The pea-shaped flowers grow along the branches like plumes. The calyx is thin, yellow, and covered with black hairs.

The seeds are cased in small hairy black pods. The flowers have a nutty scent.

When very young the leaves of the seedling gorse are soft and hairy, but gradually they become sharp spines and lose their leaf-like appearance altogether.

The stem is thick, woody, tough, and grooved.

Ulex: Lat. name of some kind of shrub.

Europaeus: 'European,' as the plant is found all over western Europe.

BROOM
Cytisus Scoparius

Found: Commons and heaths, dry places.   Common in Britain.   *Flowers:* Spring and early summer.   *Height:* 3–5 ft.

Do not confuse with *Furze* or *Gorse* (p. 92).   The easy distinction is in the leaves which clothe the stem of the *Broom*, but which in the *Furze* are sharply pointed spines.

The *Broom* is a shrub, much branched, the pea-shaped flowers growing on short stalks in long leafy spikes.   They have a pleasant scent.   The seed pods are 1½–2 in. long and black; they explode to scatter the seed.

The lower leaves have short stalks and are made up of three small leaflets, the upper ones have no stalks.

The stem is wiry, grooved, woody, and tough, and the branches are like switches in growth.

Cytisus: The Latin name for the shrub.
Scoparius. Lat., 'sweeper,' because brushes and brooms are made from this plant.

BLACK MEDICK
Medicago lupulina

Found: Waste ground, edges of cultivated fields, dry places. *Flowers:* The whole summer. *Height:* Spreading 1–2 ft. long.

Something like *Hop Trefoil* (p. 96), but notice the difference in the seed cases, which are here not wrapped in the withered flowers, and are black and strongly veined, a snail-like shape and spirally twisted. The small flowers grow in round crowded heads in spikes. The plant is covered with soft hairs.

The leaves are cut completely into three, rounded and finely toothed, tapering to short stalks, which have pointed stipules.

The stem branches from the base and spreads on the ground. The flower stems are very slender.

Medicago: From Gk. *Mēdikē,* 'Median,' applied to a kind of clover that came from Media.
Lupulina: From *lupus,* Lat. name for the hop plant.

TALL MELILOT
Melilotus altissima

Found: Fields, hedgerows and waysides, bushy places. Southern England and east coast of Ireland. *Flowers:* Summer. *Height:* 2–4 ft.

Small pea-shaped flowers grow in sprays on one side of the stem only, close together, and slightly drooping. The tall flower stems spring from the axils of the leaf stalks. The seed pod is black when it is ripe, hairy, and marked with net-like veins.

The leaves have long stalks and are cut into three narrowly oval leaflets with toothed edges. There is a pair of leaflets (stipules) at the foot of the leaf stalk, so narrow as to be like bristles.

The stem is tall and erect, slender, and branching in an upright direction.

When dried the plant has a sweet scent. It is much favoured by bees.

Melilotus: From Gk. *meli,* 'honey,' and *lōtos,* 'clover.'
Altissima: Lat., 'tallest.'

95

PEA FAMILY
Leguminosae

HOP TREFOIL
Trifolium campestre

Found: Dry fields and grassy places. Common in England, rare in northern Scotland. *Flowers:* All the summer. *Height:* Runs along the ground or rises to 6 in.–1 ft.

Something like *Black Medick* (p. 94) but distinguished by the way the seeds are carried, and the flowers do not grow in spikes.

Between thirty and fifty tiny flowers grow in crowded round or egg-shaped heads at the end of thread-like, leafless stalks which spring from the leaf axils. As the petals wither and turn downwards, the heads become brown and look like small hops. The seed pods are covered by the withered petals. The lower part of the head withers before the upper, which remains yellow.

The leaves are cut into three, the centre leaflet slightly further apart from the other two. There are small pointed stipules at the base of the flower stalks.

The stem is slender, hard, much branched from the base, spreads along the ground, and throws up erect downy flower stalks.

Trifolium: Lat., 'three-leaved.'
Campestre: Lat., 'growing in flat country.'

BIRD'S-FOOT TREFOIL
Lotus corniculatus

Found: Fields, commons, downs.   Common throughout Britain.   *Flowers:* All the summer.   *Height:* 6 in.–18 in.

Sometimes known as *Lady's Slipper*.

The pea-shaped flowers grow in spreading horizontal heads of five to ten and are tinged with red.   The brown seed pods are about 1 in. long, and also spread out like the claws of a bird's foot.

The leaflets are not the usual trefoil shape, but oval and pointed, and sometimes narrow.

The flower stalks are longer than those of the leaves.   The stems trail and branch on the ground, the flower stems rising from them.

Lotus: Lat. from the Gk. *lōtos*, 'a kind of clover.'
Corniculatus: Lat., 'in the form of a horn,' because of the shape of the seed pods.

97

KIDNEY VETCH or LADY'S FINGERS
Anthyllis Vulneraria

Found: Dry fields, hills, and stony places. All over Britain. *Flowers:* Early summer. *Height:* 6–18 in.

The pea-shaped flowers grow in pairs in dense heads (up to $1\frac{1}{2}$ in. across) at the head of branched stems, surrounded by narrow leafy bracts. The flowers are often tinged with red.

The leaves from the root are each cut into one long end leaflet and usually two pairs of quite small leaflets below. Those from the stem are long, and cut into pairs of narrow leaflets with an end one only slightly larger than the others.

The stem spreads and rises erect, and it, and the whole plant, is covered with silky hairs.

Anthyllis: From Gk. *anthullis*, the name of some flower.
Vulneraria: Lat., 'used for curing wounds.'

HORSESHOE VETCH

Hippocrepis comosa

Found: Fields, banks, chalky hilly districts. Common in some parts of England and extends to southern Scotland. *Flowers:* Spring and summer. *Height:* 6 in.–1 ft.

Very like *Bird's-foot Trefoil*, but smaller and paler, and the pods are very different. The flowers grow in spreading heads at the end of long slender stems, usually five to eight together. The jointed twisted pods are about 1 in. long, rough, with notches on their inner edges, and fine pointed tips; they grow in a flattened cluster.

The leaves are cut into four to eight pairs of small oval leaflets, with one terminal leaflet.

The stems branch from the base, and may spread along the ground.

Hippocrepis: Gk. *hippos,* 'horse,' and *krēpis,* 'shoe,' referring to the shape of the pods.

Comosa: Lat., 'hairy.'

MEADOW VETCHLING
Lathyrus pratensis

Found: Fields, hedge banks, grassy roadsides. Common in Britain.
Flowers: All the summer. *Height:* Straggling and climbing 1–2 ft.

Sometimes called *Yellow Pea* or *Meadow Pea*.

The pea-shaped flowers grow in bunches or loose spikes at the end of slender leafless stalks, about six to ten together. The larger upright petal has fine pencil lines on it. The seed pods are smooth and black.

The leaves are divided into two leaflets; a tendril, by which the plant climbs, springs from between them. They are narrow, lance-shaped, and pointed. Two leaflets (stipules) grow from the axil of the leaf stalk and the main stem. These are arrow-headed in shape, and as large or broader than the divided leaves. The 'barbs' of the arrow overlap the stem. The plant has a bunchy and leafy look.

The stem is weak, much branched, smooth, and more or less climbing.

Lathyrus: From Gk. *lathuros*, name of a kind of pulse.
Pratensis: Lat., 'growing or found in meadows.'

HERB BENET

Geum urbanum

Found: Shady banks, edges of woods, roadsides. Common in England, Ireland, and southern Scotland. *Flowers:* Summer. *Height:* 1–2 ft.

Sometimes called *Wood Avens*.

The star-like flowers ($\frac{1}{2}$ in. across) grow singly or in small clusters at the head of the stalk, with conspicuous pointed bracts between each of the five petals. When the flowers wither the fruits develop short, reddish, bristly hairs, hooked at the tip, which catch in passing objects and so disperse the seeds.

The root leaves have long stalks and are curiously divided, the broad end leaflet is large, lobed, and toothed, the two lower leaflets quite apart and very small. The stem leaves are cut into three leaflets, one much bigger than the others. This is a leafy-looking plant.

The stem is hard, hairy, rounded, and branched.

Geum: From Gk. *geuein*, 'to give a relish,' from the clove-like smell and taste of the root.

Urbanum: Lat. 'of towns,' where the plant was sometimes found.

101

WATER AVENS
Geum rivale

Found: Damp or shady places, woods, ditches, marshes. Common in Britain, except south-west England. *Flowers:* Summer. *Height:* 1–2 ft.

Three or four flowers droop at the head of the stem. They are globular in shape, each with a maroon-coloured hairy calyx divided into five pointed parts, and these clasp the flower itself, which is bell-shaped. The petals closely overlap, rather squarely ended.

When the flower has faded a rounded hairy head takes its place, and stands upright instead of drooping.

The leaves mostly grow from the root and are softly hairy, cut into three, with one much larger end leaflet. All are coarsely toothed On the leaf stalk are two pairs of small-toothed leaflets. The stem leaves are small, have short stalks, and are usually cut into three.

The stem is hard and upright, tinged with red, slender and hairy.

Geum: From Gk. *geuein*, 'to give a relish,' from the clove-like smell and taste of the root.
Rivale: Lat., 'of the brook.'

102

CINQUEFOIL

Potentilla reptans

Found: Waste places, edges of woods, grassy places. Common in England and Ireland, much less so in Scotland. *Flowers:* Summer and autumn. *Height:* Creeping, sometimes several feet long.

The flowers look like small buttercups (about 1 in. across), and the plant grows like a carpet. Do not confuse with *Silverweed* (p. 106), the leaves are quite different, and are distinctive, cut into five, spreading like a fan from the centre.

The stem is very slender and red and lies on the ground. It is much branched and roots at the nodes.

Potentilla: Lat. 'powerful,' from the supposed medicinal qualities of allied plants.

Reptans: Lat., 'creeping.'

TORMENTIL

Potentilla erecta

Found: Moors, dry fields, open woods. Common in Britain. *Flowers:* Summer. *Height:* A few inches.

Compare with the *Cinquefoil* (p. 103), which it much resembles, but the flowers are smaller ($\frac{1}{2}$ in. across) and have only four petals, so set apart from one another that when opened flat each flower has a distinct shape of a Maltese cross. They grow at the end of very slender stalks. The plant is not prostrate like the *Cinquefoil*, but more erect.

The stem leaves are also different, stalkless, and usually cut into three deeply divided toothed leaflets, with toothed leafy stipules as well, so that at first sight it appears as if there were a pair of delicate leaves growing round the stem. The lower leaves often have stalks.

The stem is erect and very slender; it forks and is finely hairy.

Potentilla: Lat., 'powerful,' because of the supposed medicinal qualities of allied plants.

Erecta: Lat., 'upright.'

SPRING CINQUEFOIL
Potentilla verna

Found: Hilly places. Not very common in England or Scotland, and not found in Ireland. *Flowers:* Spring and summer. *Height:* 6–8 in. or prostrate.

The flowers are smaller than those of the *Cinquefoil* (*Potentilla reptans*) (p. 103) and are only ½ in. across, growing at the end of short weak stems. It is often a hairy plant, but varies much.

The lower leaves grow on long stalks, cut into five or seven oblong toothed leaflets spreading out from the centre. The upper leaves may be stalkless or very shortly stalked.

The stems are weak and often prostrate, but they do not root like the *Cinquefoil*.

Potentilla: Lat., 'powerful,' from the supposed medicinal qualities of allied plants.

Verna: Lat., 'pertaining to spring.'

SILVERWEED
Potentilla Anserina

Found: Roadsides, grass verges, stony places. Common in Britain.
Flowers: Summer. *Height:* Creeps and roots.

The flowers (about ¾–1 in. across) grow at the end of slender stalks, the five petals rather open and spread out. Compare with *Cinquefoil* (p. 103), a plant it much resembles. But the leaves of *Silverweed* are deeply cut and about 9–15 in. long, the leaflets growing alternately, toothed or almost fringed, with tiny leaflets between them. They are silky and a silvery white underneath, a distinctive feature.

The stem is long, round, and sometimes red; it creeps and roots. The flower stalks rise from the creeping stem.

Potentilla: Lat., 'powerful,' from the supposed medicinal qualities of allied plants.
Anserina: Lat., 'of or pertaining to geese,' either because geese are fond of the plant or because it grows on commons frequented by them.

BITING STONECROP

Sedum acre

Found: Chalk downs, rocks and cliffs, old walls, sandy places.   Common in Britain.   *Flowers:* Summer.   *Height:* A few inches.

This smooth plant grows in dense masses or tufts, the short flower stems curving upwards from the main stem, which lies on the ground. The flowers have five pointed petals, and grow together at the head of the stalk.

The leaves are not like ordinary leaves at all.   They are thick and fleshy, egg-shaped, and grow closely pointing up the stem with no stalks, so that they make the stem look more like a spur.

The stem branches.   The plant is biting to the taste and very bitter.

Sedum: Lat., 'house-leek,' probably connected with *sedere*, 'to sit,' from the way the plant grows closely amongst stones.

Acre: Lat., 'sharp,' because of the plant's biting acid taste.

GOLDEN SAXIFRAGE

Chrysosplenium oppositifolium

Found: Wet places in woods, near streams, marshy places. Common in Britain. *Flowers:* Spring and early summer. *Height:* Creeping, with upright shoots of a few inches.

Rather inconspicuous small flowers (about $\frac{1}{6}$ in. across) that grow in flat clusters, half hidden by leaves at the branched top of the stem. The flowers have no petals, but the calyx broadens into four parts.

The leaves are rounded and grow in pairs on short stalks up the stem, crowding together at the top to form a leafy cluster on which the flowers seem to lie.

The stem creeps and roots, throwing up flowering stems.

Chrysosplenium: From Gk. *chrusos,* 'gold,' and *splēn,* 'spleen,' as the plant was supposed to be a cure for diseases of the spleen.

Oppositifolium: Lat., 'opposite leaved.'

FENNEL
Foeniculum vulgare

Found: Coastal districts, cliffs, dry banks near the sea. Fairly common in England, but not in the north or in Ireland. *Flowers:* Late summer and autumn. *Height:* 2–3 ft.

Tiny yellow flowers of the 'umbrella' family, which grow in flat heads on their branched stems.

The leaves are so finely cut as to look like threads. It is rather a waxy kind of plant and the heads are very open.

The stems are tall, shining, and slightly grooved, and are much branched. The plant has a strong smell of aniseed.

Foeniculum: From Lat. *foenum,* 'hay,' from the smell of the leaf.

Vulgare: Lat., 'common.'

SAMPHIRE

Crithmum maritimum

Found: Rocks, cliffs, near the sea. Common in the south and west of England and southern Ireland. Rare in the north and rarely found in western Scotland. *Flowers:* Summer. *Height:* 8 in.–1 ft.

The plant is rubbery and thick, much branched and smooth, with a bluish-green 'bloom' on it. The umbrella-like flat heads have a distinctly yellow appearance, though the petals of the tiny flowers are actually whitish. It is the ovaries that are yellowish and show up more than the petals.

The leaves are very deeply cut into narrow spear-shaped rubbery leaflets, which have rather a pleasant aromatic scent when crushed. They have sheath-like stalks.

The stem is round and very smooth, much branched and growing out from the root, which is usually wedged in a crack in a rock or stone, and rather woody.

Crithmum: From Gk. *krēthmon,* the name of the plant.

Maritimum: Lat., 'of the sea or sea-coast.'

WILD PARSNIP
Pastinaca sativa

Found: Waste ground, banks, field edges. Fairly common in England up to as far north as Durham. *Flowers:* Summer. *Height:* 2–3 ft.

Another of the few plants in this family that are yellow, most of them being white, and the *Parsnip* has the usual flat head with clusters of tiny flowers, in this case widely open clusters. The fruits are flat and oval, with ridges and margins.

The lower leaves are large and stalked, rather downy underneath and divided into three or more pairs of shiny toothed leaflets, spaced apart, the end leaflet being cut again into three. The leaf stalk ends in a kind of winged sheathing. The upper leaves are smaller and simpler.

The main stem is stout, hollow, downy, and grooved.

The long tap root has long been cultivated as a garden vegetable.

Pastinaca: From Lat. *pastinum*, 'a three-pronged dibble used for setting plants.'
Sativa: Lat., 'cultivated.'

ALEXANDERS

Smyrnium Olusatrum.

Found: Waste ground, especially near the sea, roadsides, at the foot of walls and ruins. Common in England and southern Scotland. *Flowers:* Spring and early summer. *Height:* 2–4 ft.

A yellowish-green plant that grows in masses, the flower heads in dense flat clusters at the top of tall coarse stalks. The fruit is oval, hard, and brown.

The lower leaves are very large, shining, and cut into three main divisions, divided again into three, with waved and toothed edges. The upper leaves are simpler. The base of each lower leaf stalk widens into a broad white or pinkish-green striped membrane, like an envelope enclosing the flower stalk, part of the leaf stem itself.

The main stem is stout, solid, furrowed, and much branched.

This is one of the first of the *Umbelliferae* to flower in the spring.

Smyrnium: From Gk. *smurna*, a synonym of *murra*, alluding to the smell of myrrh, which is common to many plants of this family.

Olusatrum: From Lat. *olus,* 'pot-herb,' and *ater,* 'black.'

112

MOSCHATEL
Adoxa Moschatellina

Found: Damp places, shady woods, undergrowth.   Common in Britain rare in Ireland.   *Flowers:* Spring.   *Height:* 4–6 in.

A low-growing weed that carpets the ground with small heads of usually five pale greenish-yellow little flowers, which grow at the end of fragile stalks.   The yellow stamens add to the pale-yellow effect. The flowers each back on to one another, the top one lying flat on the others which form the sides, as it were, of the little box-shaped head. The head turns into a green and fleshy kind of little berry.

The root leaves are cut into three leaflets, which are again divided into three notched lobes, giving a light and fern-like effect, and have long stalks.   Each flower stem has a pair of small leaves half-way up.

The stems are upright, square, soft, pinkish, and fragile.

The plant has a musky smell.

Adoxa: Gk., 'without glory,' as the plant is small and insignificant.
Moschatellina: From Gk. *moschos,* 'musk.'

113

CROSSWORT

Galium Cruciata

Found: Hedgebanks, copses, shady places. Common in England and southern Scotland. Rare in Ireland.
Flowers: Spring and early summer.
Height: 6–18 in.

Compare with *Lady's Bedstraw* (p. 115) but the flowers are larger and the leaves very different.

The leaves are egg-shaped, pointed and hairy, arranged crosswise, pointing the same way as those in the ring above. The flowers grow in rings amongst the four leaves.

The stem is square and hairy, weak, and though erect inclined to bend over and trail.

Galium: From Gk. *gala*, 'milk,' because some plants of this group were used to curdle milk for cheese-making.

Cruciata: Lat., 'cross-shaped.'

LADY'S BEDSTRAW

Galium verum

Found: Banks, fields, sandy and dry places.
Common in Britain. *Flowers:* The whole
summer. *Height:* 6–15 in.

Compare with *Crosswort* (p. 114).

Tiny four-petalled flowers grow in
clusters on short stalks which spring in
pairs from a ring of fine needle-like
leaves. The effect is that of a yellow
spike of flowers.

The leaves are small, almost grass-
like, and grow in rings of six to eight
up the stem. They are narrow, pointed,
and end in hard tips.

The stem is fragile and branched,
square and downy.

Galium: From Gk. *gala*, 'milk,' because
some plants of this group were used to
curdle milk for cheese-making. The milk
from cows which have eaten this plant
when in full flower quickly turns sour.

Verum: Lat., 'true.'

GOLDEN ROD

Solidago Virgaurea

Found: Woods, hillsides, stony places. Common in Britain. *Flowers:* Summer and autumn. *Height:* 1–3 ft.

The flowers grow at the upper part of the tall stem, giving the appearance of a golden leafy spike or spray.

The leaves from the root are narrow and stalked, while those growing from the stem are lance-shaped and slightly toothed, tapering at their base, and becoming smaller as they near the top.

The stem is hard and woody, stiffly erect and round; it can be hairy or smooth.

Solidago: From Lat. *solidare,* 'to make sound,' an account of the reputed efficacy of the plant for healing wounds.

Virgaurea: From Lat. *virga,* 'a rod,' and *aurea,* 'golden.'

116

COMMON CUDWEED
Filago germanica

Found: Dry fields, stony and sandy waysides. Common in England and Ireland, less so in Scotland. *Flowers:* The whole summer. *Height:* 6–8 in.

Rather curious little flowers growing on a grey-looking plant, covered with cottony down. The stem either ends in the round cluster of flower heads, or else branches just below the cluster, so that this looks as if it were closely packed into the fork. The head is a yellowish brown.

The leaves are small, lance-shaped, and pointed, and rather pressed againt the stem, giving it a clothed effect.

The stem is slender and upright, branching and forking.

Filago: From Lat. *filum,* 'a thread,' because the plant is covered with cottony hairs.

Germanica: Lat., 'German.'

E   117

COMMON FLEABANE

Pulicaria dysenterica

Found: Marshy places, banks of streams, damp fields. Common in southern England and Ireland, less so in the north, and rare in Scotland. *Flowers:* Summer and early autumn. *Height:* 1–2 ft.

Flat-headed yellow daisy-like flowers (1 in. across) with centres darker than the ray petals. Three or more grow at the heads of branched stems. This is a grey-looking plant with a pleasant scent, and is velvety to the touch.

The leaves are much waved, long and pointed, and clasp the stem, with arrow-shaped points. They are wrinkled and downy, the undersides woolly and grey. The plant is very leafy.

The stem is ribbed, woolly, grey, and hard.

Pulicaria: From Lat. *pulex,* 'a flea,' because the old herbalists believed the scent of the plant was disliked by fleas and insects.

Dysenterica: From Gk. for 'dysentery,' an illness for which the plant was once said to be a remedy.

NODDING BUR-MARIGOLD

Bidens cernua

Found: Ditches, marshy places. Common in England and southern Scotland. *Flowers:* Summer and autumn. *Height:* 1–2 ft.

The flower heads are about ½–1 in. across, and droop at the head of tall stems. They have a circle of narrow leafy bracts below them, spreading out like a collar.

The leaves have no stalks and are narrowly lance-shaped, but not divided, with coarse toothed leaves, those in pairs joining together round the stem.

The stem is erect and stout.

Bidens: 'Having two teeth,' from Lat. *bi-*, 'double,' and *dens*, 'a tooth, because there are two stiff bristles on each fruit.

Cernua: Lat., 'nodding,' 'drooping.'

119

CORN MARIGOLD
Chrysanthemum segetum

Found: Cornfields. Common in Britain. *Flowers:* Summer and autumn. *Height:* 1 ft.

A weed of the cornfields, having handsome golden heads which can be as large as 2 in. across, with daisy-like petals and a large deeper golden centre. The heads grow at the end of long stalks, and have a pleasant aromatic scent.

The leaves grow alternately up the stem, and the upper ones clasp it; the lower leaves are stalked.

The stem branches and grows erect.

Chrysanthemum: From Gk. *chrusos,* 'gold,' and *anthemon,* 'flower.'
Segetum: Lat., 'of the cornfields.'

RAYLESS CHAMOMILE

Matricaria suaveolens

Found: Fields, waste places, sea coasts. Fairly common in Britain.
Flowers: The whole season.   *Height:* 6 in.–1 ft.

A low-growing branched plant with a strong aromatic scent.   The flowers are curious, as there are no white petals (see *Wild Chamomile*, p. 44) but only yellow heads that look like small pincushions.

The leaves are finely cut, giving the plant a bushy, leafy appearance.
The stem is erect, furrowed, and much branched.

Matricaria: From Lat. *matrix*, 'womb,' because the plant was thought to be good for uterine diseases.

Suaveolens: Lat., 'sweet-smelling.'

121

TANSY

Tanacetum vulgare

Found: Waysides, edges of fields, banks of streams. Generally over Britain. *Flowers:* End of summer. *Height:* 2–3 ft.

The flat button-shaped heads grow at the end of branched stalks in large clusters. They look as if all the petals have been pulled off. The plant has a strong aromatic scent, and is exceedingly bitter to the taste.

The leaves are fern-like, deeply cut, and sharply toothed and smooth. They grow thickly on alternate sides of the stem and give the plant a bushy appearance.

The stem is tough, stout, erect, and somewhat purplish and ribbed. It can be slightly downy or smooth.

Tanacetum: A corruption of the Gk. word *athanasia,* 'immortality.'
Vulgare. Lat., 'common.'

COLTSFOOT
Tussilago Farfara

Found: Poor ground, waste places, damp or clay soil. Common in Britain. *Flowers:* Early spring. *Height:* 3–6 in. Varies.

One of the earliest spring flowers, sometimes looking like a yellow carpet, as the flowers bloom before the leaves appear. They grow at the tops of short stalks, forming daisy-like heads with finely narrow petals, which wither into soft, white, hairy heads. The flowers tend to close at night or in cold weather.

The leaves all spring direct from the root, which creeps along the ground, often in a dense matted growth. They are stalked and very broad, heart-shaped, with toothed and scalloped edges and covered underneath with cobwebby downy hairs.

The flower stalks are hollow and clasped by long woolly scales. They grow in tufts from the root.

Tussilago: From Lat. *tussis,* 'a cough,' because the plant was used to cure diseases of the chest. The leaves have been used as a substitute for tobacco.

Farfara: From *farfarus,* the Lat. name of the plant.

123

GROUNDSEL
Senecio vulgaris

Found: Cultivated and waste ground.   Very common throughout Britain.
Flowers: All the year round.   *Height:* 6 in.–1 ft.

A very common garden weed.   The flowers grow in close clusters, and are small and tubular, with seldom any rayed petals.   They turn into fluffy seed-bearing heads.

The leaves are much cut up and ragged-looking, with narrow toothed lobes, stalkless, and half clasping the stem.   They are very smooth, and grow alternately up the stem.

The flower stalks spring from the axils of leaf and stem.   The stem is shining and has often a reddish tinge, and can be quite smooth or with cottony hairs.   It can be densely white or woolly.

Senecio: From Lat. *senex*, 'old' or 'aged,' because of the hoary look of some of this genus.
Vulgaris: Lat., 'common.'

VISCID GROUNDSEL

Senecio viscosus

Found: Waste places. Not very common, but local in England, Ireland, and southern Scotland. *Flowers:* Summer and autumn. *Height:* 6–18 in.

Distinguished from *Groundsel* by having thirteen conspicuous rayed petals, the flowers growing in loose clusters. Also by having sticky, strong-smelling hairs all over the plant. When they wither the flowers turn into fluffy heads, and the seeds are blown away in the wind.

The leaves are more deeply cut than the common *Groundsel*, and their lobes more jagged.

The stem is hard, sticky, and branched.

Senecio: From Lat. *senex*, 'old' or 'aged,' because of the hoary look of some of this genus.

Viscosus: Lat., 'sticky.'

*E   125

OXFORD RAGWORT
Senecio squalidus

Found: Noticeably on walls and railway embankments.   It has spread much on bombed sites, where the dry rubble provides a home like its native lavas of Mount Etna.   Middle and southern England, and Ireland.   *Flowers:* Summer and autumn.   *Height:* 6 in.–1 ft.

Not a native plant, and first established on Oxford walls.   The flower-heads, about ¾ in. across, grow in a loose cluster, with black tips to the bracts of the involucre.   It has eight rayed flowers.

The bright green leaves usually grow only on the stem, half clasping it with ears, smooth, deeply and narrowly lobed, and rather thick. The stem is erect and rather loosely branched.

Senecio: From Lat. *senex,* 'old' or 'aged,' because of the hoary look of some of this genus.

Squalidus: Lat., 'coarse' or 'rough.'

126

RAGWORT
Senecio Jacobaea

Found: Dry and neglected land, roadsides, waste ground.   Very common in Britain.   *Flowers:* Summer and autumn.   *Height:* 2–3 ft.

Daisy-like brilliant yellow flower heads (about ¾ in. across) grow in fairly close branched clusters at the tops of branching stalks.   The plant often grows in masses on waste farm land or cliffs by the sea, and looks like a sheet of gold.   It is a strong leafy plant.

The leaves growing from the root are deeply cut and coarsely toothed, the end lobe much the largest.   They are usually smooth, but sometimes downy on the underside.   The stem leaves are stalkless, much cut, with small wings where they clasp the stem.

The stem is erect, angled, tough, branched, and rather reddish.

Senecio: From Lat. *senex,* 'old' or 'aged,' because of the hoary look of some of this genus.

Jacobaea: Lat., 'belonging to James,' another name for the plant being *St. James's Wort.*

127

SMALLER-FLOWERED GOAT'S-BEARD

Tragopogon minor

Found: Fields and meadows. Common in Britain. *Flowers:* Early summer. *Height:* 1–2 ft.

Sometimes called *John-go-to-bed-at-noon*.

The long pointed green bracts are twice as long as the flower head and stick out like rays. The flower heads grow singly at the top of tall stalks and are rather like *Dandelions* (p. 134) and flat-headed. They wither into handsome feathery heads bearing the seeds, and the wind blows them away. Because the flowers open at dawn they tend to close about midday.

The lower leaves can be as long as 8 in. and are smooth and clasp the stem, growing to a long narrow point, almost grass-like. The upper leaves are shorter. The stem is very upright.

Tragopogon: From Gk. *tragos*, 'he-goat,' and *pōgōn*, 'beard,' because of the feathery beard-like seed-bearing head.
Minor: Lat., 'lesser.'

OX-TONGUE
Helminthia echioides

Found: Waste places, field edges, shady hedge banks.   Dispersed over England and south-east Scotland, rare in east Ireland.   *Flowers:* Summer and autumn.   *Height:* 1–3 ft.

Do not confuse with the *Sow-thistle* (p. 133).

This is a coarse, bristly plant, covered with stiff, almost prickly hairs which are often hooked, and which each have a whitish swelling at the base.

The flower heads grow in irregular crowded clusters, and each grows out of a rounded involucre made up of five pointed heart-shaped bracts, each with a flattened base, giving a leafy look to the flower head.   The rayed petals are strap-shaped, and the flowers turn into fluffy seed-bearing heads.

The root leaves are lance-shaped, with bristly edges, stalked, coarsely toothed, and very rough.   The stem leaves are heart-shaped and clasp the stem.

The stem is stout, much branched, bristly, and full of a bitter milky juice.

Helminthia: From Gk. *helmins,* 'a tapeworm,' from the supposed likeness of the seed to the shape of a worm.

Echioides: Gk., 'viper-like.'

129

COMMON HAWKBIT

Leontodon autumnalis

Found: Waste places, fields.   Throughout Britain.   *Flowers:* Late summer
and autumn.   *Height:* 6–18 in.

Rather like the *Cat's-ear* (p. 131), but the flowers are smaller and
the leaves narrower.   The flower head grows at the end of a long
flower stalk, which is swollen just below the head.

The leaves grow in a rosette on the ground and are long and narrow,
with coarse teeth or lobes, very variable and either smooth or with a
few long stiff hairs.

The stems are erect, usually branched with one or two single heads
of flowers, and leafless.

Leontodon: From Gk. *leōn*, 'lion,' and *odous*, 'tooth,' because of the shape
of the leaves.

Autumnalis: Lat., 'of the autumn.'

LONG-ROOTED CAT'S-EAR

Hypochaeris radicata

Found: Fields, grassy places. Common in Britain. *Flowers:* Summer and autumn. *Height:* 6–18 in.

Compare this plant with the *Dandelion* (p. 134) and the *Hawkweed* (p. 136).

The flower stalk springs from the centre of a circle of leaves flat on the ground. The flower-heads grow singly at the top (over 1 in. across), and are encased in layers of closely overlapping bracts. The rayed petals are strap-shaped, cut like a fringe into five teeth. The flowers wither into a feathery head, and the seeds are carried away by the wind. The rayed petals close soon after being picked.

The leaves are rough and hairy on both sides, with broad jagged teeth pointing slightly backwards. There are no stem leaves.

The stem usually divides into several long flower stalks, and is hairy below but smooth above, and slightly grooved.

Hypochaeris: Gk. name for the plant.

Radicata: Lat. 'possessing a tap root.'

WALL LETTUCE
Lactuca muralis

Found: Old walls, shady places, stony banks.   Not uncommon in England;
in Perthshire and Stirlingshire in Scotland, but found only in Co. Wicklow
and Co. Louth in Ireland.   *Flowers:* Summer.   *Height:* 1–2 ft.

A tall slender plant, much branched, with loose open clusters of
small flower-heads, about ½ in. long.

The leaves are deeply cut into widely toothed lobes, the end lobe
broadly triangular.   The upper stem leaves are narrower, and taper
into 'wings' which form part of the stalk, and clasp the stem with
pointed ear-shaped bases.   The leaves are thin, smooth, sometimes
tinged with red and bluish green underneath.

The stem is slender, smooth, and branched.

Lactuca: Lat., 'lettuce.'
Muralis: Lat., 'found on walls,' from *murus*, 'wall.'

132

COMMON SOW-THISTLE

Sonchus oleraceus

Found: Waste ground and fields. Common in Britain. *Flowers:* The whole season. *Height:* 2–3 ft.

A common weed. The flowers are not more than 1 in. across. They grow in short clusters, and are a paler yellow than many of the similar-looking flowers in this large family. When the flowers wither a tuft of white hairs sticks out of the elongated green cup or involucre.

The leaves are shining, crisp, and clasp the stem with long arrow-shaped ears; they are slightly prickly and sharply toothed. The lower leaves are deeply divided.

The stem is hollow, thick, smooth, and full of a milky juice. It divides into three to six short flower stalks at the top.

Sonchus: Lat. name of the plant.
Oleraceus: Lat., 'herb-like.'

DANDELION

Taraxacum officinale

Found: Waste places, roadsides, cultivated ground, fields.   Very common in Britain.   *Flowers:* Throughout the season.   *Height:* 6 in.–1 ft.

A very common weed.   The flower heads are large and grow singly at the top of the stalk.   The rayed petals are strap-shaped, square-ended, and finely cut into five tiny points.   After flowering the head turns into a fluffy ball and the seeds blow away.

The leaves are toothed or notched, often like the broad teeth of a saw, the lobes generally pointing downwards.   They spring from the root, growing like a plate, flat on the ground, and are smooth.

The flower stem stands erect and grows up from the centre of the leaves; it is hollow and full of a milky, bitter juice, and is leafless.

Taraxacum: The medieval Lat. name, probably of Arabic or Persian origin.
Officinale: From Lat. *officina*, 'workshop,' because the plant was used by the old herbalists.

SMOOTH HAWK'S-BEARD

Crepis capillaris

Found: Waste ground, edges of fields, walls. Common in Britain. *Flowers:* Summer and autumn. *Height:* 1–3 ft.

Daisy-like little flower heads, which are somewhat bell-shaped in bud. Compare with others in this family such as *Nipplewort* (p. 137). The flowers grow in loose open clusters, and are only about ½–¾ in. across. They wither into white, silky, seed-bearing heads.

The lower leaves are lance-shaped, and can be as long as 9 in. They are irregularly and rather jaggedly toothed and smooth. The stem leaves are few and have no stalks, and are narrowly arrow-shaped, clasping the stem on either side with long points.

The stem is erect and branched, slender and furrowed.

Crepis: From Gk. *krēpis,* 'a slipper,' from some fancied likeness to the shape of a slipper.

Capillaris: Lat., 'hairlike,' because of the thin flower stalks.

MOUSE-EAR HAWKWEED
Hieracium Pilosella

Found: Commons, banks, dry pastures, and walls. Very common in Britain. *Flowers:* The whole season. *Height:* 6 in.

Lemon-coloured flowers looking rather like small dandelions, which are tinged with red at the tips of the undersides of the petals. The flower heads tend to close in the afternoon.

The leaves grow in a spreading ring from the root, the flower stalk rising from the centre. The leaves keep close to the ground, and are rather like mouse ears, narrow and spoon-shaped, with long hairs on the upper surface, downy and white underneath.

The stem is stiffly erect, slender, and leafless. The plant spreads by means of runners.

Hieracium: From Gk. *hierax,* 'a hawk,' because according to writers of ancient times the hawk 'was wont to quicken his sight' by using the juice of the plant.

Pilosella: Lat., *pilosus,* 'hairy,' and *-ella,* 'little.'

NIPPLEWORT

Lapsana communis

Found: Waste places, fields, and walls.   Common in Britain except in the extreme north of Scotland.   *Flowers:* Summer and autumn.   *Height:* 1–2 ft.

A common weed.   Small flower-heads—$\frac{1}{4}$ in. across—grow in loose upright clusters, each set in an oval cup-shaped involucre.   The rayed petals are strap-shaped.   The flower-heads close in wet weather.

The lower leaves are stalked, broadly egg-shaped, with lower small narrow pointed segments from the same mid-rib.   They are thin and hairy, with scalloped tooth-like edges.   The upper leaves are much smaller, lance-shaped, with distantly toothed edges, and are not stalked.

The stem is round, branched, tough, hairy, and hollow.

Lapsana: From Gk. *lapsanē,* 'charlock.'
Communis: Lat., 'common.'

PRIMROSE

Primula vulgaris

Found: Banks, open woods, fields.   Common in Britain.   *Flowers:* Spring.
Height: 3–4 in.

Too well-known to need description, this is perhaps the favourite of all spring flowers. It has a delicate scent, and the pale flowers grow on slender stalks which spring from a short stout central stem, hidden by leaves.

The leaves are soft and wrinkled, with a network of veins underneath, and have soft hairs.

The slender stems are downy and a pale pink.

Primula: Diminutive from Lat. *primus,* 'first.'
Vulgaris: Lat., 'common.'

138

COWSLIP

Primula veris

Found: Open fields and downs.   Common in England and Ireland.   Rare in Scotland.   *Flowers:* Spring.   *Height:* 3–6 in., but can be as much as 10 in. in long grass.

Each flower is cased in a pale green tube or sheath (calyx) and is tubular, widening into a rounded cup, each petal notched with an orange mark at its base.   The flowers grow in close drooping clusters and are sweetly scented.

The leaves are like those of the *Primrose* (p. 138), wrinkled and roundly toothed, but tend to narrow quite sharply half-way down, so that the stalk becomes, as it were, winged.   On dry ground they can be almost stalkless and lie in a tuft.

The stem is round and downy.

Primula: Diminutive from Lat. *primus,* 'first.'
Veris: Lat., 'of the spring.'

OXLIP

Primula elatior

Found: Copses and chalky meadows in eastern counties of England. *Flowers:* Early spring. *Height:* 6 in.–1 ft.

This is the true *Oxlip* and is very like what is called the hybrid or the *False Oxlip*. The latter is a cross between the *Primrose* (p. 138) and the *Cowslip* (p. 139), and usually found where these two flowers are growing together. The true *Oxlip* is a distinct species.

The calyx is covered with long hairs, is smaller, and the flowers are widely bell-shaped, and of a pale primrose yellow. A distinguishing feature between the two is the thickening at the mouth of the corolla tube in the hybrid flowers, not seen in the true *Oxlip*.

The leaves have winged stalks, and are wrinkled and toothed.

The stalk is thick and long like that of the *Cowslip*, bearing the flowers at its head, each on a short branched stem.

Primula: Diminutive from Lat. *primus*, 'first.'
Elatior: Lat., 'taller.'

YELLOW LOOSESTRIFE
Lysimachia vulgaris

Found: Damp shady places, river banks, marshes. Frequent in England, local in Ireland, rare in Scotland. *Flowers:* Summer. *Height:* 2–3 ft.

The flowers (about ½ in. across) grow in clusters on short stalks from the axils of the leaves, forming a leafy spike. They are shortly tubular opening into five parts, with orange dots in the centre.

The leaves are broadly lance-shaped and grow in pairs or sometimes in rings of three or four up the stem, stalkless and with plain edges, and hairy beneath.

The stem is stiff, more or less downy, branched, and springs from a creeping rootstock.

Lysimachia: After Lysimachus, King of Thrace, who was said to have discovered a plant of this kind.

Vulgaris: Lat., 'common.'

141

MONEYWORT or CREEPING JENNY

Lysimachia Nummularia

Found: Damp shady places, copses, banks. Not uncommon in England, south of Durham. *Flowers:* Summer. *Height:* Prostrate, trails to 1–2 ft.

Handsome golden flowers ($\frac{3}{4}$–1 in. across) grow on short stalks in the leaf axils, usually singly but occasionally in pairs. There are five cuplike petals, joined at the base.

The leaves grow along the stem in pairs, and are rounded with plain edges. They have short stalks and are smooth and of a bright green.

The stem lies on the ground in trails, rooting at the nodes.

Lysimachia: After Lysimachus, King of Thrace, who was said to have discovered a plant of this kind.

Nummularia: From Lat. *nummulus*, diminutive of *nummus*, 'money,' from the round leaves.

YELLOW PIMPERNEL

Lysimachia nemorum

Found: Woods, shady places, copses. Throughout Britain. *Flowers:* All the summer. *Height:* Lies on the ground.

Sometimes called *Wood Loosestrife.*

This is a smooth plant of a pale yellowish green, which sometimes carpets a patch of woodland.

The five-petalled flowers grow singly at the end of the threadlike stems (about ½ in. across).

The leaves grow in pairs, are oval, smooth, and pointed with very short stalks. They are rather shiny, and paler below than above.

The stem is slender, reddish, and often roots as it lies on the ground, gradually rising a few inches.

Lysimachia: After Lysimachus, King of Thrace, who was said to have discovered a plant of this kind.

Nemorum: Lat., 'of the woods.'

143

YELLOW-WORT
Blackstonia perfoliata

Found: Chalky places, downs, heaths, dry fields. Rather local in England south of Westmorland, and in Ireland. *Flowers:* Summer. *Height:* A few inches to 1 ft.

Sometimes called *Yellow Centaury*. It has the same smooth look as the *Centaury* (p. 240), with a 'bloom' on it. The flower has eight petals and grows in loose, open-branched clusters.

The root leaves are spoon-shaped and grow in a rosette at the foot of the stem. The stem leaves are in pairs and completely joined together, so that the main stem seems to pierce them. They are a pale bluish green.

The stem is very upright and stiff, round, a pale green, tough, and branched.

Blackstonia: After John Blackstone, a London apothecary, who died in 1763.
Perfoliata: Lat. *per*, 'through,' and *foliatus*, 'leaved,' meaning 'pierced through the leaf,' a feature of the stem as described above.

LARGE-FLOWERED MULLEIN

Verbascum virgatum

Found: Edges of fields, waste places. Rare in England.
Flowers: Summer and autumn.
Height: 2–4 ft.

There are a number of *Mulleins*, often thought to be introduced, and not truly wild. This one is very hairy and extremely handsome, with its long plume of golden flowers (1–1½ in. across) crowded on to a strong tough upright stem. It has no branches, and stands up conspicuously erect. The stamens are clothed with woolly purple hairs. The bracts are pointed and overlap the buds.

The big root leaves may be 3 in.–1 ft. long, oblong and slightly toothed.

The plant is covered with short hairs.

Verbascum: Lat. for 'mullein.'
Virgatum: Lat., 'twiggy.'

YELLOW TOADFLAX

Linaria vulgaris

Found: Hedges, field verges, cornfields. Common in Britain except the Scottish Highlands. *Flowers:* Summer and autumn. *Height:* 1–3 ft.

Very like Snapdragon flowers, but with a longer spur or tail.   The rounded part of the lower lip is a deep orange colour, and is divided into three.   It quite closes the tube in which the nectar is found, and only long-tongued bees can get at this. The flowers grow in a long loose spike.

The leaves, which give the plant a lightly leafy appearance, are long, smooth, and very narrow, almost hair-like.   They have a bluish tinge, and grow thickly up the stem.

The stem is upright and stiff.

Linaria: From Lat. *linum*, 'flax,' because the leaves of some plants of this group resemble those of Flax.

Vulgaris: Lat., 'common.'

146

MONKEY-FLOWER
Mimulus guttatus

Found: Damp places, banks of streams, ditches.   In many parts of Britain, especially in Scotland.   *Flowers:* All the summer.   *Height:* 1–2 ft.

Sometimes called *Yellow Mimulus.*

The flowers are large and showy (over 1 in. across), each with a broad tube and lips cut into broad lobes.   The throat and undersides are marked with small red dots.   The flowers grow in short spikes, springing from the leaf axils.

The leaves are egg-shaped, stalkless, and grow in pairs; they are coarsely toothed, smooth, and clasp the stem.

The flower stalks are 2 in. long or more.   The main stem is erect and usually smooth.

Mimulus: Lat., 'a little mime,' alluding to the gaping, masklike corolla.
Guttatus: Lat., 'dotted or spotted as if by drops.'

147

YELLOW RATTLE
Rhinanthus minor

Found: Fields, grassy roadsides.　Common in Britain.　*Flowers:* Summer.
Height: 6–18 in.

A wiry plant.　A conspicuous pale green calyx encloses each flower, shaped like a double sea-shell or like a bladder, with flat sides and a pointed toothed mouth.　The small flowers are tubular, with two lips, the upper one arched like a hood, and the lower one spread out and divided into three.　There is often a purple spot on one or both lips.　The stamens are hidden inside and have blue tips.　The flowers grow up the stem and are stalkless, giving the effect of a loose, leafy spike.　When they wither and dry the seeds rattle inside the pods.

The leaves grow in pairs, are stalkless, lance-shaped and narrow, and sharply toothed, as if fringed.

The stem is square, slender and branched, and often streaked with purple.

Rhinanthus: From Gk. *rhis,* 'nose,' and *anthos,* 'flower,' because of the shape of the upper lip of the flower.
Minor: Lat., 'lesser.'

148

COMMON COW-WHEAT
Melampyrum pratense

Found: Woods, dry copses, and heaths. Common in Britain. *Flowers:* Summer and autumn. *Height:* 6 in.–1 ft.

You may think at first that this plant is one of the *Vetches*, but the flowers are not pea-shaped. They grow in pairs, pointing in the same direction, where the leaf joins the stem. Each has a two-lipped mouth, the lower lip is three-lobed and sticks out, the upper lip turns back. The seeds are black, and shaped like grains of wheat.

The leaves also grow in pairs, and are very narrowly lance-shaped and almost stalkless.

The stem is upright, with widely forking branches.

Melampyrum: From Gk. *melas,* 'black,' and *puros,* 'wheat.'
Pratense: Lat., 'growing in meadows.'

YELLOW ARCHANGEL
Lamium Galeobdolon

Found: Copses, hedgerows, shady places. Fairly common, but more especially in southern England and the east of Ireland. Not found in Scotland. *Flowers:* Spring and early summer. *Height:* 1–2 ft.

One of the *Dead-nettles*, and compare also with *Black Horehound* (p. 261). The plant is also called *Weasel Snout*.

The tubular little flowers (the upper and lower lips so distinctive a feature of this family) grow in rings where the leaves join the main stem, and so look like a flowery spike. Each flower has a tall arched lip like a hood, with the curved stamens inside. The lower lip is divided into three pointed parts, streaked with brown.

The leaves grow in pairs on short stalks, and are oval, stalked, toothed, and pointed.

The stem is square and hairy, erect and unbranched.

Lamium: Lat. for *Dead-nettle*, from the same Gk. stem as *lamia*, 'a monster,' referring to the odd appearance of the flower.
Galeobdolon: From Gk. *galē*, 'weasel,' because the shape of the flower is like a weasel's face, and *bdolon*, 'bad smell.'

WOOD SAGE

Teucrium Scorodonia

Found: Dry woods, stony banks, thickets. Common in Britain.
Flowers: Summer and autumn.
Height: 1–2 ft.

Sometimes called *Wood Germander*.

Tubular little flowers of a greenish yellow, with pinkish red stamens that stick straight out beyond the flower. The lip is much longer than the lower upper and hangs down. The flowers grow in pairs in a long one-sided narrow spike, usually 5–6 in. long.

The leaves are soft to the touch, wrinkled and downy, and grow in pairs. They have short stalks and rounded teeth. The pair of leaves just below the flower spike is stalkless.

The stem is upright, hard, and almost woody at the foot, hairy, and of a reddish-brown colour.

The plant has a pleasant aromatic scent like that of the garden variety.

Teucrium: From Gk. *teukrion*, the name of the plant.

Scorodonia: From *skorodon*, Gk. name for garlic.

DAPHNE FAMILY
Thymeleaceae

SPURGE LAUREL
Daphne Laureola

Found: Woods, copses, damp and shady places. Not uncommon in England, unknown in Ireland. *Flowers:* Spring. *Height:* 2–4 ft.

Really a shrub, with flowers growing in clusters at the head of the stem in the axils of the leaves, which are bunched together. The flowers are tubular and have no real petals. They open four-cleft mouths with bright yellow centres, which eventually turn into bluish-black poisonous berries. The flowers are sweet-scented.

The leaves are evergreen, bright, shining, leathery, and tough. They are sharply pointed and almost stalkless, and grow only at the head of the stem in a crown.

The stem is upright, brown, and leafless except for the branched leaves at the top.

Daphne: The classic laurel, into which the nymph Daphne was changed.
Laureola: Lat., 'a little laurel crown,' because of the crown of leaves at the head of the plant.

PORTLAND SPURGE
Euphorbia portlandica

Found: Sandy coasts, on cliffs near the sea, stony wastes. Southern and western English coast up to Galloway in Scotland, and in Ireland. *Flowers:* Summer and autumn. *Height:* A few inches to 1 ft.

A bushy little plant with bluish-green leaves which cluster thickly up the stem. The latter branches to fork again into pairs of short flower stalks at the leaf axils. The flower heads are of the usual Spurge type (see *Wood Spurge*, p. 154), with a small cup of bracts joined together to enclose both male and female flowers.

The stem leaves are narrow and pointed, those growing in pairs on the flower stalks almost join. They have a bluish 'bloom' though a pale green, but are not thick and leathery.

The stem is tough but not very stout, woody at the base. The flower stems are slender.

Euphorbia: After Euphorbus, physician to Juba, King of Mauretania, who was said to have used plants of this family in medicine.

Portlandica: Lat., 'native to the Isle of Portland.'

153

WOOD SPURGE

Euphorbia amygdaloides

Found: Woods and copses, shady places. Common in England except in the north, and unknown in Scotland. *Flowers:* Spring. *Height:* 1–2 ft.

The Spurges are all curious-looking shrub-like plants, and this one stands out in woods and copses and undergrowth in early spring with its plumes of clear yellow-green flowers. They grow at the head of dark red woody stems, and are like round flat saucers, with no true petals. What are called floral leaves grow in pairs and are joined together in a kind of flat cup. The whole effect is leafy and yellow in contrast to the dark green of the lower leaves.

The leaves are grouped closely together towards the middle of the stem, lance-shaped and oblong. The upper ones are shorter.

The stem is woody, tough, a dark red, and branches from the base, often in two tall stems. It and the leaves have a bitter milky juice.

Euphorbia: After Euphorbus, physician to Juba, King of Mauretania, who was said to have used plants of this family in medicine.
Amygdaloides: Gk., 'almond-like.'

WILD HOP
Humulus Lupulus

Found: Hedgerows, thickets. Over most of England. *Flowers:* Summer.
Height: Twines to great lengths.

There are two kinds of flowers—male flowers growing on one plant
and female on another. The male flowers grow in loose clusters and
are quite small. They have no real petals but five yellowish sepals.
The female flowers are the rounded heads we usually associate with
hops. The bracts closely overlap each other like scales, and each
bract has a tiny flower in its axil. After flowering the rounded head
becomes much larger.

The hop is cultivated for its seeds, which are like little nuts hidden
under the bracts. The seeds are bitter and used for the making of beer.

The leaves are rough and grow opposite each other, stalked, coarsely
toothed, and deeply cut into three or five lobes.

The stalks are very tough, thin, long and twining, and tightly clasp
the trees or bushes over which they rapidly climb.

Humulus: Medieval Lat. name, from Old German *humela*, 'hops.'
Lupulus: From *lupus*, Lat. name for the hop plant.

BIRD'S-NEST ORCHIS
Neottia Nidus-avis

Found: Damp woods and amongst dead leaves. Not common but found in many parts of England, Ireland, and southern and central Scotland. *Flowers:* Spring and early summer. *Height:* 9–18 in.

A rather dense spike of flowers (3–4 in. long), which are a yellowish-brown with deeply cleft lips.

There are no leaves, but the stem is sheathed with brownish scales which replace them.

The roots are a mass of thickened fibres, unlike ordinary roots, and nourish the plant from decayed leaf-mould (chiefly beech leaves).

Neottia: Gk., 'bird's nest,' referring to the matted roots.

Nidus-avis: Lat. *nidus*, 'nest,' and *avis*, 'of a bird.'

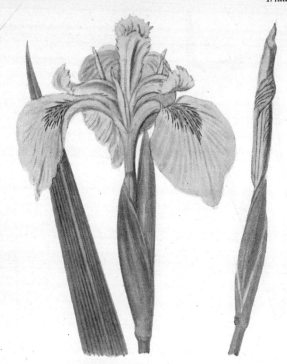

YELLOW FLAG
Iris Pseudacorus

Found: River banks, ditches, marshes. Common in Britain. *Flowers:* Summer. *Height:* 2 ft.

A stiffly erect plant with large flowers, each in a sheathing bract, the sepals broad and spreading downwards.

The leaves are stiff, very upright, and sword-shaped.

The stem is stiff and erect.

Iris: Gk., 'rainbow,' and for some sweet-smelling plants, perhaps the Yellow Flag.

Pseudacorus: From Gk. *pseudo-,* 'false,' and *akoros,* 'the Sweet Flag.'

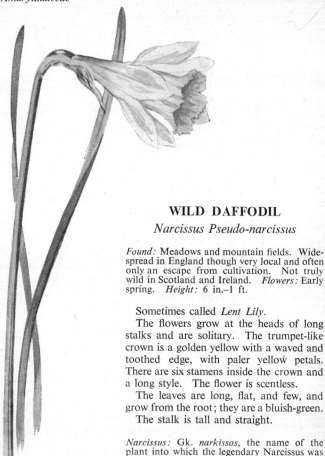

WILD DAFFODIL

Narcissus Pseudo-narcissus

Found: Meadows and mountain fields. Widespread in England though very local and often
only an escape from cultivation. Not truly
wild in Scotland and Ireland. *Flowers:* Early
spring. *Height:* 6 in.–1 ft.

Sometimes called *Lent Lily*.

The flowers grow at the heads of long
stalks and are solitary. The trumpet-like
crown is a golden yellow with a waved and
toothed edge, with paler yellow petals.
There are six stamens inside the crown and
a long style. The flower is scentless.

The leaves are long, flat, and few, and
grow from the root; they are a bluish-green.

The stalk is tall and straight.

Narcissus: Gk. *narkissos*, the name of the
plant into which the legendary Narcissus was
transformed.

Pseudo-narcissus: From Gk. *pseudo-*, 'false
i.e. not the real narcissus.

4

BLUE FLOWERS

SWEET VIOLET
Viola odorata

Found: Sheltered banks, woods, under hedges. Common in the south and east of England, and in the east of Ireland. *Flowers:* Early spring. *Height:* 2–4 in.

This flower can also be white, and is the only scented wild violet.

There are five petals, the lowest lengthens out in a short hollow spur. There are also five blunt sepals. A pair of small bracts grows half-way up the flower stem.

The leaves are heart-shaped with rounded or slightly pointed ends, and small rounded teeth; they are downy and have long stalks, and grow larger after the flower has flowered. They grow from the root, which usually gives off creeping runners, from which flower and leaf stalks also spring.

The stems are slender and smooth.

Viola: The Lat. name for 'violet.'
Odorata: Lat., 'sweet-smelling.'

WOOD VIOLET
Viola Riviniana

Found: Woods and copses, banks. Common in Britain. *Flowers:* Spring and early summer. *Height:* 6 in. or more.

There are two Wood Violets in Britain: *V. Riviniana* and *V. Reichenbachiana*. The latter has narrower flowers with less widely veined lower petals, a coloured (never whitish) spur without a kink at the end, and less rounded leaves.

V. Riviniana is very like the *Sweet Violet* (p. 160) but scentless, usually paler in colour, the sepals pointed, broader petals, and usually a whitish spur, though it is sometimes violet.

The leaves grow in a rosette from the short root stock, from which leafy flowering stems branch, the stems growing much longer than those of the *Sweet Violet* as the season goes on.   The leaves are heart-shaped and pointed, the stems are slender and smooth.

Viola: The Lat. name for ' violet.'
Riviniana: From Rivin, an eighteenth-century botanist.

WILD PANSY

Viola tricolor

Found: Valley grasslands in hilly country. Not very abundant in Britain.
Flowers: Spring to autumn. *Height:* Up to 1 ft.

Sometimes called *Heartsease*. This plant varies considerably, The
flowers can be purple, whitish, or yellow, or the colours may be mixed
together. Compare with *Field Pansy* (p. 89), and note how the two
upper petals of the *Wild Pansy* stand upright.

The leaves are stalked, egg-shaped with blunt or rounded teeth,
and the stipules are large, much cut, and leafy.

The stem is branched, angled, and straggling.

Viola: Lat. name for 'violet.'
Tricolor: Lat., 'three-coloured.'

162

COMMON MILKWORT
Polygala vulgaris

Found: Heathy places, meadows, and fields. Common in Britain. *Flowers:*
All the summer. *Height:* 2 in.–1 ft.

A tough little plant, inconspicuous amongst grass. The flowers are
usually blue, but may be lilac, purple, pink, or even white. They are
rather more tubular than bell-shaped, and hang on tiny stalks from
the main stem in loose spikes. Each flower has five sepals which
closely resemble petals, the two inner being larger than the outer.
The petals are joined to the stamens.

The leaves are smooth, lance-shaped, and small, and grow alternately up the stem.

The stem varies in height and is slender and upright.

Polygala: Gk. *polu,* 'much,' and *gala,* 'milk,' because the root is full of
a milky juice.
Vulgaris: Lat., 'common.'

163

COMMON FLAX

Linum usitatissimum

Found: Near cultivated fields, waste places. Various parts of England. *Flowers:* Summer. *Height:* 12–18 in.

In Britain this is only found as a weed of cultivation. The flowers, which grow in loose clusters at the head of the stem, are a rich blue with rounded overlapping petals.

The leaves grow alternately up the stem, and point upwards, smooth, pointed, and varying much in breadth.

The stem is very slender and wiry, erect and smooth, slightly bunched at the top.

Linum: Lat., 'flax,' the plant from which linen is woven.

Usitatissimum: Lat. 'very much in use.'

164

MEADOW CRANE'S-BILL

Geranium pratense

Found: Damp meadows, roadsides. Fairly common in Britain and southern Scotland. Very rare in Ireland. *Flowers:* Summer. *Height:* 2–3 ft.

A handsome bright blue-purple flower (1¼ in. across) with five petals which are finely veined and tend to fall easily. The flowers, in loose clusters, usually grow in pairs. The seed pods are conspicuous, long, and sharply pointed and hanging down.

The leaves are really round, but so finely cut that they hardly appear so. They are hairy and usually cut into seven or nine parts, notched deeply again. The root leaves are long stalked, the stem leaves stalkless.

The stem is tall, upright, downy, and branched.

Geranium: From Gk. *geranos*, 'a crane,' because the seed has a long beak which looks like the bill of a crane.

Pratense: Lat., 'growing in meadows.'

165

TUFTED VETCH

Vicia Cracca

Found: Hedges and bushy places.   Common in Britain.   *Flowers:* Summer.
Height: 2–5 ft.

Bright purplish-blue pea-shaped little flowers (about $\frac{1}{2}$ in. long) grow
in spikes, and hang down on one side of the stem.   They vary in
number, about ten to thirty in a spike.   Each flower has a tiny foot-
stalk, the main flower stalk being several inches long.   When the
flower withers a brown pod forms, about 1 in. long, with six to
eight seeds.

The leaf is cut into many pairs of leaflets, the midrib ending in
branched tendrils by which the plant climbs.   The leaf may be as
long as 4 in.

The stem is angled, branched, and weak.

Vicia: Lat., 'a kind of pulse, perhaps vetch.'

Cracca: Lat. name for 'wild vetchling.'

166

SEA HOLLY
Eryngium maritimum

Found: Sandy seashores.   Common in England, Ireland, and southern Scotland.   *Flowers:* Late summer.   *Height:* 1–2 ft.

A rather unexpected member of the 'umbrella' family, and the only one that is blue; the plant looks more like a thistle.

The flowers grow in a dense round head without any of the usual spoke-like footstalks common to this family.   The head is ringed by stiff, spiny, prickly bracts.

The stem leaves clasp the stem and are very stiff, cut into short lobes with coarse, sharp, prickly teeth and much veined.   The root leaves are large, 2–5 in. across, and almost round, with the same hard tough spines.

The stem is smooth, stout, upright, and branched.

The whole plant—leaves and stem—has a bluish waxy 'bloom' on it, like so many sea plants, and is very smooth.

Eryngium: From Gk. *ērungion*, diminutive of *erungos*, 'sea holly.'
Maritimum: From Lat. *mare*, 'sea,' i.e. found near the sea coast.

LAMB'S LETTUCE
Valerianella olitoria

Found: Cornfields, banks, waste places. Fairly common in Britain.
Flowers: Spring and summer. *Height:* 6 in.–1 ft.

Sometimes known as *Corn Salad*.

Tight little clusters of pale bluish flowers grow at the head of forked stalks, conspicuously enclosed in green bracts like a cup.

The leaves from the stem are a pale green, narrow and oblong, and grow in pairs; they are slightly toothed near the base, and sometimes clasp the stem.

The stem is slender, slightly angled, soft, and juicy. It forks continuously.

Valerianella: Possibly from Lat. *valere*, 'to be healthy,' because of the supposedly healing qualities of the plant.

Olitoria: Lat., 'belonging to the kitchen garden.'

DEVIL'S-BIT

Scabiosa succisa

Found: Fields, heaths, meadows.   Common in Britain.   *Flowers:* Summer and autumn.   *Height:* 12–18 in.

Rounded heads of tiny flowers grow like small pin-cushions at the end of stiff stalks.   The flower heads are surrounded by several rows of green bracts.   The stamens are conspicuous.

The lower leaves are stalked, hairy, usually with plain edges, and broadly lance-shaped.   The stem leaves grow opposite each other and become more and more narrow up the stem.

The stem is erect and branches above and is slender.   The rootstock is short, and looks as if it had been bitten off.

Scabiosa: Lat. 'rough,' 'scurfy,' from *scabies*, 'the itch.'
Succisa: Lat., 'cut off,' in allusion to the root (see above).

FIELD SCABIOUS
Knautia arvensis

Found: Cornfields, waysides, fields. Common in Britain, except in northern Scotland. *Flowers:* All the summer. *Height:* 1–3ft.

The large lilac-blue heads of flowers grow at the end of long stalks, usually in threes, the middle stalk of the three being the longest. The flower heads are about 1½ in. across, and are made up of numerous small flowers, the outer ones having larger petals than the others, and the inner flowers being slightly reddish in colour. The effect is of a fringe of petals on the edge of the cushion-like centre.

The leaves from the root are stalked and coarsely toothed, but they vary much, and are lance-shaped. The stem leaves grow in pairs and are stalkless, and may be slightly lobed or all may be deeply cut and coarsely toothed. All are hairy.

The stem is hollow and upright, round, hairy, and branching.

Knautia: After Knaut, a German botanist.
Arvensis: Lat., 'of the fields.'

170

CORNFLOWER
Centaurea Cyanus

Found: Cornfields. Formerly common, now rare in Britain. *Flowers:* Summer. *Height:* About 2 ft.

A cornfield weed. The bright blue flowers grow at the tops of upright stalks in crowded heads, the outer ring of flowers, five-toothed, larger than those in the centre, and a brighter blue. The rounded involucre below the flower-head is made up of tight rows of little scales with fringed brown edges.

The lower leaves are long, narrow, and pointed, with deep notches. The upper leaves have no stalks, are very narrow, and not cut or toothed. They are covered with a woolly down.

The stem is thin, ribbed, upright and branched, and covered with woolly hairs.

Centaurea: From the classic fable that the centaur, Chiron, cured a wound in his foot by applying some such plant to it.

Cyanus: Lat. form of Gk. *kuanos*, name of some dark blue mineral.

171

SUCCORY or **WILD CHICORY**

Cichorium Intybus

Found: Dry places, roadsides, chalky districts.   Fairly common in England and Ireland.   Rare in Scotland.   *Flowers:* Summer and autumn.   *Height:* 1–3 ft.

A wiry, angular-looking plant, with handsome heads of blue flowers that grow, stalkless, two or three together on the main stem, or singly on the branched stems.   The tiny florets are crowded together, square-ended, and fringed.

The leaves clasp the stem with pointed wing-like bases, and are hairy and toothed.   The root leaves lie spread in a circle on the ground, and are shaped rather like those of the *Dandelion* (p. 134), with backward-pointed coarsely toothed lobes.

The stem is very tough, almost like a slender twig, and branches widely.   It is grooved and hairy.

Cichorium: Lat. form of *kichorion*, Gk. name of the plant.
Intybus: Lat. name of the plant.   (Note that 'endive' is a corruption of this.)

NETTLE-LEAVED BELL-FLOWER
Campanula Trachelium

Found: Copses and hedgerows.   Not uncommon in some parts of southern
England.   *Flowers:* Summer and autumn.   *Height:* 2–4 ft.

Sometimes called the *Nettle-leaved Campanula*.

A tall handsome plant, the bell-shaped flowers growing in leafy
clusters at the head of the stem, usually three or four together, though
single flowers sometimes grow on short stalks.   The flowers are cut
into five lobes, about ¾ in. across and 1 in. long, and are each encased
in a pointed hairy calyx; the upper buds of the cluster open first.

The lower root leaves are broadly heart-shaped, toothed, and
bristly.   They have longer stalks than the upper stem leaves, which
are narrower, and taper to a point, the more so as they near the
flower clusters.

The stem is upright, hairy, angular and rough, and usually a deep
red on two sides and green on the other.

Campanula: Lat., 'a little bell.'
Trachelium: From Gk. *trachēlos*, 'the neck,' because the plant was reputed
to have healing qualities for diseases of the throat.

HAREBELL

Campanula rotundifolia

Found: Heaths, dry high fields, banks, turfy places.   Common in Britain.
Flowers: Summer and early autumn.   *Height:* 6–12 in.

This is the 'Bluebell of Scotland.'   (Compare with the *Bluebell* or *Wild Hyacinth*, p. 194.)

The flowers are delicately bell-shaped, cut into five broadly pointed lobes, and droop gracefully at the head of slender stalks.   They grow singly or in loose clusters, and blow in the wind.

The leaves from the stem become narrower and more grass-like the higher they are.   Only those from the root (which soon wither away) are round or heart-shaped.

The stem is slender and wiry.

Campanula: Lat., 'a little bell.'
Rotundifolia: Lat., 'with rounded leaves.'

174

LESSER PERIWINKLE
Vinca minor

Found: Woodland banks, hedgerows, shady places.   Widespread in Britain.
Flowers: Spring and early summer.   *Height:* Trails.

A trailing plant.   The flower petals are joined together in a broad
tube and then divide into five rather square-ended parts.   At the
opening of the tubular 'mouth' are white marks, like a central white
ring.

The leaves grow in pairs, and are evergreen, shining, smooth, and
narrowly egg-shaped.

The stem is long and trailing, smooth and reddish.   It branches
and roots.   The flower stalks spring upright from the main trailing
stem.

Vinca: From Lat. *vincire*, 'to bind,' in allusion to the plant's winding and
trailing habit.
Minor: Lat., 'lesser.'

JACOB'S LADDER
Polemonium caeruleum

Found: Bushy places, chiefly in the north of England.   *Very rare.*   *Flowers:* Summer.   *Height:* 18 in.–2 ft.

This plant is very often cultivated in gardens, and in consequence it is often found as an escape as it seeds easily.

The flowers are handsome and grow in clusters at the head of the stem.

The root leaves grow in tufts with stalks of about 6 in., cut into a number of narrow lance-shaped leaflets.   The stem leaves are few and small, and rather feathery.

The stem is erect.

Polemonium: Lat. form of *polemōnion*, Gk. name for Greek Valerian.
Caeruleum: Lat., 'sky-blue.'

VIPER'S BUGLOSS

Echium vulgare

Found: Waste ground, chalky or gravelly places. Throughout Britain, specially southern England; rare in Scotland. *Flowers:* All the summer. *Height:* 1–2 ft.

A brilliantly handsome plant, the flowers growing in a long spike made up of short clusters, purple-red in bud and bright blue when open. The flowers are tubular, opening into five parts.

The leaves from the root are stalked, long and rough, and covered with stiff hairs. The stem leaves are lance-shaped.

The stem is upright with stiff hairs. The whole plant is rough and bristly.

Echium: From Gk. *echis*, 'viper,' some say because the plant was a cure for the bite of a viper, others refer the name to the shape of the flower.

Vulgare: Lat., 'common.'

FORGET-ME-NOT

Myosotis palustris

Found: Wet places, by streams and ditches.   Common in Britain.   *Flowers:* The whole summer.   *Height:* 6–18 in.

The flowers grow in loose clusters on curved slender stalks, each with a five-pointed calyx, and with a central yellow eye.   The plant tends to grow in masses or beds.

The leaves are narrowly spoon-shaped, stalkless from the stem, stalked from the root.

The stem varies, and may be stout or weak, covered with fine hairs or smooth..   It lies on the ground and then rises erect.

Myosotis: From Gk. *muosōtis*, 'mouse's ear,' from the shape of the leaves.
Palustris: From Lat. *palus*, 'marsh.'

SMALL BUGLOSS
Lycopsis arvensis

Found: Fields, waste places. Common in Britain. *Flowers:* Summer.
Height: 1–2 ft.

A rough, bristly plant. The flowers grow in clusters with leafy
bracts; they are tubular, curved, with five opening lobes, and about
¼ in. across. At the base of each petal at the top of the tube is a
white scale, giving a conspicuous white centre to the flower.

The stem leaves are stalkless, lance-shaped, and covered with
bristles. They clasp the stem and the margins are waved.

The stem is branched and rough.

Lycopsis: From *lukopsis*, Gk. name for a plant which has been identified
with bugloss.
Arvensis: Lat., 'of the fields.'

179

EVERGREEN ALKANET

Anchusa sempervirens

Found: Waste ground, banks, and roadsides. Not particularly common but scattered over Britain, probably not truly wild except perhaps in south-west. *Flowers:* Spring and summer. *Height:* 1–2 ft.

Bright blue flowers (about ⅔ in. across) with conspicuous white centres and five rounded petals. They grow in one-sided short spikes on short footstalks, the main flower stems springing from the axils of the leaves with the main stem.

The leaves are broadly oval, pointed, rough and covered with coarse hairs, those from the stem with shorter stalks than those from the root. The plant is leafy-looking.

The main stem is hollow, stout, and covered with strong white hairy bristles.

Anchusa: The Lat. form of *anchousa*, the Gk. name of the plant.
Sempervirens: Lat. *semper*, 'always,' and *virens*, 'green,' because the plant remains green throughout the winter.

BORAGE
Borago officinalis

Found: Waste ground near buildings, an occasional escape. Much culti-vated as a garden plant. *Flowers:* Summer. *Height:* About 1 ft.

The handsome brilliant blue flowers (about ¾ in. across) droop in clusters at the head of long stems. The anthers form a conspicuous purple-black cone in the centre of the flower. The whole plant is covered with bristly hairs. It smells of cucumber.

The lower leaves are stalked, oval, and pointed; the upper much narrower and stalkless, narrowing into ears where they join the main stem.

The stem is erect, branched, and bristly.

Borago: From the medieval Lat. *borrago*, which probably comes from an Arabic word meaning 'source of sweat,' from the medical use to which it was put.
Officinalis: From Lat. *officina*, 'workshop, because the plant was used by the old herbalists.

FIGWORT FAMILY
Scrophulariaceae

BUXBAUM'S SPEEDWELL	**GERMANDER SPEEDWELL**	**COMMON SPEEDWELL**
Veronica persica	*Veronica Chamaedrys*	*Veronica officinalis*

BUXBAUM'S SPEEDWELL

Found: Waste and cultivated places, common in Britain.   *Flowers:* Spring and summer.   *Height:* Lies on the ground.

The small, bright blue flowers grow singly on short stalks from the axils of the leaves. They have conspicuous white centres, and the sepals are usually longer than the petals. The flowers are about the same size as those of the *Germander Speedwell*.

The leaves are rather more oval than heart-shaped, coarsely toothed, and stalked.

The stems are prostrate, those of the flowers very slender.

GERMANDER SPEEDWELL

Found: Woods and fields, banks, roadsides. All over Britain. *Flowers:* Spring and summer. *Height:* About 1 ft.

The flowers spring from the leaf axils. They are a bright blue, and grow in spikes on stalks longer than the leaves. The four petals open widely from a little tube and are about $\frac{1}{2}$ in. across. They are much paler on the undersides.

The leaves are stalkless, oval, hairy, coarsely toothed, and grow in pairs.

The stem lies on the ground at first, creeping and rooting, and then rises upright; it is hairy between each pair of leaves, on two opposite sides down the stem.

COMMON SPEEDWELL

Found: Woods, dry fields, banks. Common in Britain. *Flowers:* The whole summer. *Height:* 4–10 in.

Rather small pale blue flowers, streaked with pink, about half the size of those of the *Germander*, grow in spikes, the flower stems springing from the leaf axils.

The leaves grow in pairs, and are downy with short stalks, oval or rounded, and toothed.

The stems are much branched and lie on the ground, the branches rising. They are hairy and creep and root.

Veronica: Named after St. Veronica.

Persica: Lat., 'Persian.'

Chamaedrys: The Lat. form of the Gk. name of the plant.

Officinalis: From Lat. *officina*, 'workshop,' because the plant was used by the old herbalists.

THYME-LEAVED SPEEDWELL
Veronica serpyllifolia

Found: Damp places and roadsides, fields.   Common in Britain.   *Flowers:*
Spring and summer.   *Height:* 3–8 in.

The flowers are a very pale blue (about $\frac{1}{4}$ in. across), with dark hair-
lines on the insides of three petals.   They grow in delicate spikes,
with very short stalks or none at all.   The buds are much bluer than
the open flowers and the stamens are prominent and blue-tipped.

The leaves are small, and grow opposite each other.   They have
hardly any stalks, are oval or egg-shaped, with slight rounded teeth.
The bracts (growing at the base of each flower stalk) look like leaves,
and so make the flower spike appear quite leafy.

The stem runs along the ground, rooting, and then grows erect
and branching.

Veronica: Named after St. Veronica.
Serpyllifolia: Lat. *serpyllum,* 'thyme,' and *folium,* 'leaf,' i.e. thyme-leaved.

BROOKLIME

Veronica Beccabunga

Found: Ditches, streams, and ponds. Common in Britain. *Flowers:* The whole summer. *Height:* 1–2 ft.

The flowers grow in spikes from the leaf axils, very like other Speedwells, with white centres.

The leaves grow in pairs, shortly stalked, thick, smooth, and toothed.

The stems lie on the mud or float, and are hollow and smooth, spreading and rising.

Veronica: Named after St. Veronica.

Beccabunga: Medieval Lat. for *Bachbunge*, the German name for the plant.

185

FIGWORT FAMILY
Scrophulariaceae

| **WOOD SPEEDWELL** | **IVY-LEAVED SPEEDWELL** |
| *Veronica montana* | *Veronica hederaefolia* |

WOOD SPEEDWELL

Found: Damp woods and thickets. Most parts of England and Ireland, and in several Scottish counties. *Flowers:* Spring and summer. *Height:* Trails and then rises up to about 1 ft.

Very like *Germander Speedwell* (p. 183), but the flowers are smaller and paler, and there are fewer in the loose spike.

The leaves are larger, with distinct hairy stalks.

The hairy stem trails and roots, the flower stalks rising from it.

IVY-LEAVED SPEEDWELL

Found: Waste places, and also a weed in cultivated places; banks.   Not so common in Britain as many of the other Speedwells.   *Flowers:* All the summer.   *Height:* 6 in.–1 ft.

The bluish-lilac tiny flowers grow singly from the leaf axils, on short stalks.

The leaves are inclined to be ivy-shaped, slightly hairy and rather thick, heart-shaped but cut into five to seven large teeth or lobes, the middle one broader and rounder than the others.

The stems lie on the ground, and are much branched from the base.

Veronica: Named after St. Veronica.

Montana: Lat., 'of the mountains.'

Hederaefolia: Lat. *hedera*, 'ivy,' and *folium* 'leaf,' i.e. 'having ivy-shaped leaves.'

CLARY

Salvia horminoides

Found: Waste places, dry fields, roadsides. Scattered over England and the southern part of Ireland, but rare in Scotland. *Flowers:* All through the summer. *Height:* 1–2 ft.

This plant is a kind of sage. The flowers are small and purplish-blue; they grow in rings of about six, up the stem, forming hairy spikes. Below the flowers are heart-shaped bracts, which turn a purplish-red colour. The small flowers have two lips, the upper one hood-like. The calyx is large and bell-shaped and covers the flower tube.

The leaves are wrinkled, the lower ones stalked, oblong, hairy, and toothed. The upper leaves have no stalks, and are triangular in shape or pointedly egg-shaped; they grow in pairs and are coarsely toothed.

The stem is upright, branches slightly, and is angled and leafy.

Salvia: Lat. for 'sage,' from *salvus*, 'sound,' 'healthy.'

Horminoides: horminon, Gk. name for 'sage,' *-ides*, 'likeness.'

GROUND IVY

Nepeta hederacea

Found: Waste places, hedge banks, copse edges.   Very common in Britain.
Flowers: Spring and early summer.   *Height:* 6–18 in.

Do not connect this plant with *Ivy* (p. 60).   There is no connection between the two.

Small tubular flowers grow in rings in the axils of the leaf stalks and the main stem.   Each flower has a white centre and red spots on the flat lower lip.   It grows out of a hairy green calyx, which is half the length of the flower itself.

The leaves are stalked, hairy, round, with regular rounded teeth.

The stem is square, hard, and reddish.   It creeps along the ground and throws up the flower stalks, rooting at the nodes.

Nepeta: Named after the Etruscan town of Nepete (now Nepi).
Hederacea: Lat., 'ivy-like' (in habit and shape).

SELF-HEAL
Prunella vulgaris

Found: Fields, hedge-banks, waste places. Very common in Britain.
Flowers: Early summer and autumn. *Height:* 6–12 in.

The small tubular flowers grow in short dense spikes (gradually lengthening out to 1 or 2 in.), each flower with an upper lip bending over the lower one. The colour is often a bluish purple. Each ring of flowers has broad, pointed, leaf-like bracts below it, edged with purple. The calyx is tinged with red, flat, broad, and two-lipped.

The leaves grow opposite each other, are stalked, hairy, and almost without teeth. They are broadly lance-shaped.

The stem is square and slightly hairy, often tinged with red. The flower stem grows erect from a creeping and rooting rootstock.

Prunella: Perhaps from the Low Lat. *brunus,* 'brown,' an obsolete name for a throat disease, because the plant was supposed to be a cure for it.

Vulgaris: Lat., 'common.'

190

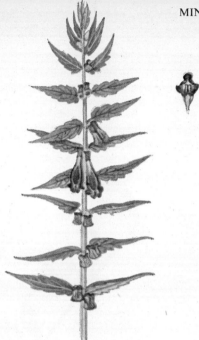

GREATER SKULL-CAP
Scutellaria galericulata

Found: Damp places, banks of streams and ditches, shady places. Fairly common in England and Scotland, less so in Ireland. *Flowers:* Late summer. *Height:* 8 in.–2 ft.

The curious bell-shaped little flowers grow in pairs in the leaf axils, and turn in the same direction, so that they hang down side by side (⅔ in. long). They are a paler blue inside than out. Each has two lips; the upper has a kind of hollow pouch at the back.

The leaves grow in pairs and have hardly any stalks. They are lance-shaped and pointed, with rounded toothed edges, and are slightly downy.

The stem branches from the base.

Scutellaria: From Lat. *scutella*, 'a little dish,' because of the shape of the calyx.

Galericulata: From Lat. *galericula*, the diminutive of *galerum*, 'a hat,' i.e. cap-shaped.

191

BUGLE

Ajuga reptans

Found: Waysides, fields, woods. Common in Britain. *Flowers:* Spring and early summer. *Height:* 4–12 in.

The little flowers are tubular and grow in close rings in the axils of the upper leaves, forming a leafy spike. The lower lip of the flower is long, spreading, and divided. The calyx is covered with long hairs.

The root leaves grow in a tuft, the flower stalk rising from the centre, at first short and club-shaped, later elongating into the long spike. The leaves are oval with roundly toothed or plain edges, smooth and stalked. The stem leaves are stalkless, narrow, and pointed. They grow in pairs, each pair at right angles to the pair above it.

The flower stem is square with sparse hairs, though very hairy, mostly towards the upper part where the flowers grow. It has purplish-blue rims to the angles of the square sides, which give it a bluish look, and the whole plant tends to look purplish as it grows older.

Long slender runners radiate from the centre of the plant and lie on the ground, rooting at the tips.

Ajuga: From Lat. *a*-, 'not,' and *jugum*, 'a yoke,' referring to the apparent absence of the upper corolla lip.
Reptans: Lat., 'creeping.'

VERVAIN
Verbena officinalis

Found: Dry wastes, roadsides. Frequent in southern England, but rare in the north and in Ireland; unknown in Scotland. *Flowers:* Summer and autumn. *Height:* 1–2 ft.

A wiry plant with tiny lilac-blue flowers growing in slender spikes, and stalkless, in the axils of small bracts.

The leaves grow opposite each other, and are lance-shaped, but deeply lobed and coarsely toothed and hairy. The upper leaves are narrower and stalkless.

The stems are four-angled, wiry, and branched.

Verbena: Lat. name for the plant, and for altar plants generally used by the Romans.

Officinalis: From Lat. *officina,* 'workshop,' because the plant was used by the old herbalists.

BLUEBELL or
WILD HYACINTH

Scilla non-scripta

Found: Woods, glades, shady places. Common in Britain.
Flowers: Spring. *Height:* 6–18 in.

The *Bluebell* of England; *Wild Hyacinth* in Scotland (see p. 174).

The narrow bell-shaped flowers hang at the top of tall stems, each with a pair of narrow bracts at the base of the little flower stalk. The mouth of the flower curls back into six points: the free ends of the six floral leaves. The buds stand upright on the stalk and only droop as the flowers open and the flower stalks lengthen. The flowers are scented and grow in dense masses, carpeting the ground.

The leaves show first, and grow close to the ground in early spring like a rosette, from the centre of which the spike of unopened buds rises. The leaves eventually grow up long and narrow sometimes over a foot high, shining and V-shaped.

The stem is round, leafless and smooth, juicy and shining.

Scilla: From Gk. *skilla,* 'squill.'
Non-scripta: Lat., 'not written,' meaning without markings, thus differing from some hyacinths.

5

RED, SHADES OF PINK,
or
PURPLE FLOWERS

COMMON
RED POPPY

Papaver Rhoeas

Found: Cornfields, waste ground.   Common in England and Ireland, less so in Scotland.   *Flowers:* All the summer.   *Height:* 1–2 ft.

Sometimes called the *Field Poppy*.

The handsome scarlet flowers can be as large as 2–3 in. across. Two of the petals are smaller than the other two; there is often a purple patch at the base of the petals, and the stamens grow in a dark ring in the centre.   The petals are soft and delicately fluted with waved edges, looking crumpled in bud, when they are enclosed in two bristly sepals.

The leaves are long and deeply cut into narrow lance-shaped segments, each ending in a sharp point.

The stems are slender and covered with stiff bristly hairs, which stick out horizontally.

Papaver: The Lat. word for poppy.
Rhoeas: From Gk. *rhoias*, 'a kind of poppy.'

COMMON FUMITORY
Fumaria officinalis

Found: Dry fields, waste places. Common in England and southern Scotland. *Flowers:* Summer and autumn. *Height:* Spreads and trails up to 1 ft.

A common garden weed. The flowers grow in loose spikes, the four little petals in pairs like a tube, the outer pair joined at the base. Each is tipped with a darker shade of red. A minute spur sticks out beyond the tiny flower stalk, so making the flower look horizontal.

The leaves are a pale green and so much divided that they look fern-like and feathery.

The stem is weak, long, and rambling, growing in a spreading tuft.

Fumaria: From Lat. *fumus,* 'smoke,' because of the light and airy look of the leaves.

Officinalis. From Lat. *officina,* 'workshop,' because the plant was used by the old herbalists.

LADY'S SMOCK
Cardamine pratensis

Found: Damp fields and meadows, sides of streams, moist places. Common in Britain. *Flowers;* Spring and early summer. *Height:* About 1 ft.

Somtimes called *Cuckooflower.*

Delicate flowers (nearly ¾ in. across), which vary in colour from white to the more usual pale lilac, while the buds are slightly deeper in tone. The petals are veined and the flowers grow in clusters at the head of the stem. The plants may grow singly or in masses in damp meadows. The seed pods are an inch or more long.

The stem leaves are smooth and so deeply cut that the leaflets seem almost needle - shaped, but the lower leaves are cut into more rounded leaflets, which grow in pairs from the midrib, and grow thickly at the foot of the plant.

The stem is smooth and upright

Cardamine: From Gk. *kardamon*, a kind of cress, as the plant belongs to that group.

Pratensis: Lat., 'growing in meadows.'

RED CAMPION

Melandrium dioicum

Found: Damp shady places, hedge banks. Common in Britain. *Flowers:* All the summer. *Height:* 2–3 ft.

The flowers grow in clusters, loosely branched near the head of the stem, on short stalks. The deeply notched petals are almost divided into two, and the flowers grow on softly hairy stems from the leaf axils. The tubular calyx is hairy, dark red, and ribbed, and narrows into five teeth at the top.

The leaves from the root are hairy, oval, and have long stalks. Those from the stem are narrower, more pointed, and clasp the stem. They grow in pairs.

The stem is covered with hairs, and forks continually above. It is swollen at the joints, and slightly sticky near the top.

Melandrium: Lat. 'honey flower,' or possibly named after an Italian botanist, Melandri.

Dioicum: From Gk. *di-*, 'two,' and *oikos*, 'house,' i.e. having stamens and pistils growing in flowers of different plants.

199

RAGGED ROBIN
Lychnis Flos-cuculi

Found: Damp places, ditches, shady places, wet fields. *Flowers:* Spring and summer. *Height:* 1–2 ft.

The ragged-looking flowers grow at the head of slender stalks, in a loose cluster. The petals are cut into four toothed and very narrow lobes, and the flowers are nearly $1\frac{1}{4}$ in. across. The calyx is a dark crimson, with ten ribs and five short teeth.

The leaves from the stem grow in pairs spaced widely apart, and are stalkless and very narrow. Those from the root are stalked, narrow, and lance-shaped.

The stem is forked, furrowed and upright, slender, slightly downy below and sticky above.

Lychnis: From Gk. *luchnos*, 'torch' or 'lamp,' because of the bright colour of the flower petals.

Flos-cuculi: Lat., 'flower of the cuckoo.'

200

CORN COCKLE
Agrostemma Githago

Found: Cornfields. Common in Britain. *Flowers:* Summer. *Height:* 2–3 ft.

Single flowers (nearly 2 in. across) grow at the head of tall leafless stems, the petals a deeper colour inside than out, but paling to white in the centre. They are joined together into a tube enclosed in a long, hairy ribbed calyx, which is divided into five long, narrow, and pointed teeth sticking out far beyond the petals like a widely pointed star.

The plant is a pale grey-green owing to the white hairs that cover it.

The leaves are long, narrow, and pointed.

The stem is erect, hard, and covered with soft hairs, with upright branching flower stems.

Agrostemma: From Gk. *agros*, 'field,' and *stemma*. 'garland' or 'wreath.'

Githago: From *gith* or *git*, Lat. name for some aromatic black-seeded plant, used in cookery in Roman times.

201

COMMON MALLOW
Malva sylvestris

Found: Waste places, waysides, edges of fields. Common in England and Ireland, less so in the north. *Flowers:* Summer. *Height:* 1–3 ft.

Large (1½ in. across) mauve-pink flowers with five petals streaked with a darker red, narrowly heart-shaped, with a cleft in the centre. The flowers grow in clusters at the axils of the leaves up the stem, on short stalks.

The leaves are broad and have long stalks, divided into five to seven lobes, the end one longer than the others, and roundly toothed. The stipules are large, pointed, and fringed with hair.

The stem grows erect and is hairy, solid, and round. The leaf stalks are hairy.

Malva: Lat. name for 'mallow.
Sylvestris: Lat., 'of the woods.'

MUSK MALLOW
Malva moschata

Found: Hedge banks, dry fields, waysides. Not uncommon in England, Ireland, and southern Scotland. *Flowers:* Late summer. *Height:* 18 in.–2 ft.

Pale rose-coloured flowers (about 2 in. across), streaked with a deeper rose, grow in clusters at the end of branched stems, usually seven or eight flowers together. The petals are dented or waved across their squarish ends (compare *Common Mallow*), and sometimes have an almost ragged look. The big hairy pale green calyx loosely holds the flower, and has five pointed sepals.

The stem leaves, which help to distinguish this plant from other Mallows, are finely cut from the centre into a number of narrow segments. The root leaves are less divided and are circular, cut into broad lobes. When crushed they have a somewhat musky smell. The whole appearance of the plant is leafy and bushy.

The stem is hollow, hairy and upright, strong and slightly branched.

Malva: Lat. name for 'mallow.'
Moschata: From Gk. *moschos*, 'musk.'

HERB ROBERT

Geranium Robertianum

Found: Stony and waste places, shady walls. Common in Britain.
Flowers: The whole summer. *Height:* 6 in.–1 ft.

A reddish plant. The bright pink flowers have five petals streaked a deeper rose. The sepals close tightly over the fruit, and are hairy with long points. The flowers tend to droop in bad weather and at night.

The leaves grow in pairs and are elaborately cut into three segments, which are again cut, giving an almost fern-like effect. They turn bright scarlet in autumn, and are slightly hairy.

The stem is much branched, hairy, and spreading. The flowering stems usually fork at the leaf axils, and also turn a bright red.

Geranium: From Gk. *geranos*, 'a crane,' because of the shape of the fruit, like the bill of a crane.

Robertianum: Possibly in allusion to Robert, Duke of Normandy, who was famous for his medical work in the Middle Ages. The plant was once used for stanching blood.

204

SHINING CRANE'S-BILL
Geranium lucidum

Found: Stony and waste places, old walls. All over Britain, but rare in northern Scotland. *Flowers:* Spring and summer. *Height:* 6 in.–1 ft.

One of the most distinctive of the Crane's-bills, with small flowers ($\frac{1}{8}$–$\frac{1}{4}$ in. across), the plant always smooth and shining. It turns red in summer. The calyx is like a wrinkled pyramid, with sharply angled edges—another distinguishing feature.

The leaves are circular, but cut into lobes that spread out like the fingers of a hand, and are bluntly toothed, smooth, and shining.

The stem is red, branched, and smooth.

Geranium: From Gk. *geranos*, 'a crane,' because of the shape of the fruit, like the bill of a crane.

Lucidum: Lat., 'shining.'

205

DOVE'S-FOOT CRANE'S-BILL
Geranium molle

Found: Waste and cultivated places, fields.   *Flowers:* The whole season.
Height: Up to 1 ft., but spreads.

The flowers ($\frac{1}{4}$–$\frac{1}{2}$ in. across) grow in pairs, from stalks springing from the axils of the leaves. They have five rather deeply notched petals; the sepals each end in a hard point. When the flower withers a small pointed green 'bill' forms from the carpels, and turns upright from the stem.

The leaves from the root are hairy, grow on long stalks, are about 1 in. across or more, and though round are deeply cut into wedge-shaped lobes that are cut again. The stem leaves are also round and covered with soft hairs but smaller; they have deeply cut and notched lobes, usually six or seven divisions. If the leaves were not so deeply cut they would be cup-like.

The stem is downy, weak and straggling, and swollen at the joints. The stems branch thickly from the central root and spread close to the ground, and are often red. The flower stems are fragile and short.

Geranium: From Gk. *geranos*, 'a crane,' because of the shape of the fruit, like the bill of a crane.
Molle: Lat., 'soft and tender.'

206

PRICKLY
REST-
HARROW

Ononis spinosa

FIELD
REST-
HARROW

Ononis repens

PRICKLY REST-HARROW

Found: Sandy dry fields, waste ground.   Common in Britain.   Not found in Ireland.   *Flowers:* Summer and autumn.   *Height:* 1 ft. or more.

A much-branched upright shrubby plant, often growing close to the ground, with sharp spines.   The pea-shaped flowers form a leafy spike, the leaflets being narrow and growing up the flower stem, giving a bushy effect.   The seed pod is the same length as the calyx.
The stem is hard, tough, woody, and a dark red.

FIELD REST-HARROW

Found: Sandy places and fields, especially near the sea.   Common in Britain.   *Flowers:* Summer.   *Height:* 1–2 ft.

Very like the *Prickly Rest-harrow*, but has seldom any spines.   The flowers are usually stalkless, or very shortly stalked.   The plant has many low spreading branches.   The leaflets are oval and blunt, with small sharp teeth, and the whole plant is covered with soft sticky hairs.

Ononis: Gk. name of plant. *Spinosa:* Lat., 'thorny.'   *Repens:* Lat., 'creeping.'

HARE'S-FOOT TREFOIL

Trifolium arvense

Found: Dry fields, cornfields, sandy places.   Common in Britain, rather more so in the south.   *Flowers:* Summer and autumn.   *Height:* 3 in.–1 ft.

A downy plant, slender and branching, with tiny flowers in soft heads, at first nearly round then lengthening to a more oblong shape, about ½–¾ in. long.   The hairy calyx teeth are longer than the petals, and so add to the feathery, almost furry, look of the heads.

The leaves are cut into three leaflets, hairy and slender.   A pair of large stipules ending in sharp points grow at the base of the leaf stalk.

The stem is much branched and more or less erect.

Trifolium: Lat., 'three-leaved.'

Arvense: Lat., 'of the fields.'

RED CLOVER
Trifolium pratense

Found: Meadows and hayfields. Abundant in Britain. *Flowers:* The whole summer. *Height:* 1 ft. or more.

The large rounded heads are made up of many little flowers which grow closely together at the top of the stalk, and are scented and produce much nectar. Each bud is enclosed in a bristly green calyx.

The trefoil leaves are oval, cut into three leaflets, which are often marked with a whitish crescent-shaped band. Two stalkless narrow leaves, cut into three, grow at the base of the flower head.

The stem is hairy, especially the upper part, with egg-shaped stipules or leaflets (about ¾ in. long) growing at the axil of the leaf stalk with the main stem.

Trifolium: Lat., 'three-leaved.'
Pratense: Lat., 'growing in meadows.'

209

SAINFOIN
Onobrychis viciifolia

Found: Limestone districts, chalk hills and downs. Southern and eastern England. *Flowers:* Early summer. *Height:* 12–18 in.

The pea-shaped flowers grow in handsome spikes, a bright pink colour veined with a deeper rose. At first the flowers are closely packed, but they lengthen, broaden, and loosen later. The calyx teeth are long and pointed. The seed pod is semicircular and edged with short teeth.

The leaves are cut into about twelve pairs of leaflets, with one end leaflet at the tip of the mid-rib. They are smooth above and there are no tendrils, though the leaves seem vetch-like.

The stem is upright, tall, strong and downy.

Onobrychis: From Gk. *onos,* 'an ass,' and *bruchein,* 'to gnaw,' because the plant is a favourite food of donkeys.

Viciifolia: Lat., 'with leaves like the vetch.'

BUSH VETCH
Vicia sepium

Found: Hedgerows, thick grass bushy places. Common in Britain.
Flowers: All the summer. *Height:* 1–2 ft.

Two to four pale purple pea-shaped flowers droop in clusters from the leaf axils. The petals are streaked with darker lines, and each flower is encased in a hairy tubular calyx. The seed pods are 1 in. long, and smooth and black. The plant tends to grow in tangled masses.

The leaves are cut into four to six pairs of oval leaflets and the leaf stalk ends in a tendril, which is usually branched, the leaflets often have pointed ends. There are small stipules at the junction of the leaf and the stem which are arrow-shaped.

The stems are weak and straggling and angular. The plant does not actually climb much.

Vicia: Lat. name for 'vetch.'
Sepium: Lat. 'of the hedges.'

CRIMSON VETCHLING
Lathyrus Nissolia

Found: Amongst grass, bushy places.
Southern England. Rare and not
known in Scotland and Ireland.
Flowers: Early summer. *Height:*
About 1 ft.

Sometimes called the *Grass Pea*
or *Grass Vetchling*.

So like grass that this plant is
difficult to discover until the
flower is out, and it is probably
not so rare as it seems. The
flowers grow singly or possibly
two together at the top of a long
stalk, and eventually wither to
form long narrow seed pods.

The leaves are grass-like, even
the leaf stalk is flattened out to
look like grass. The flower stalk
has no leaves and there are no
tendrils.

The stems branch from the
base.

Lathyrus: From Gk. *lathuros*, name
of a kind of pulse.

Nissolia: In honour of G. Nissole,
a French botanist.

TUBEROUS BITTER VETCH

Lathyrus montanus

Found: Open woods, hedges, and thickets.   Common in Britain.   *Flowers:* Spring and early summer.   *Height:* 6 in.–1 ft.

Two to four pea-shaped flowers grow in a loose spike on slender stalks.

The leaves have no tendrils, the leaf stalk ends in a fine point, or sometimes in a narrow leaflet.   The leaflets are usually in two pairs, sometimes more, and broadly lance-shaped to linear.

The stems are smooth and upright.

Lathyrus: From Gk. *lathuros*, name of a kind of pulse.

Montanus: Lat., 'belonging to the mountains.'

BRAMBLE or BLACKBERRY
Rubus fruticosus

Found: Hedges, thickets, woods, and waste places. Common in Britain.
Flowers: Summer. *Height:* Trails and branches to great lengths.

The flowers grow in clusters at the ends of branches, with five pale
pink or mauvish-white petals. The fruit is the succulent blackberry
we know so well.

The leaves are divided into three oval leaflets, a shining green above
and dull underneath, stalked, and with small hooked prickles up the
underside of the midrib.

The stems are covered with downward-pointing prickles, and can
be quite stout as they branch and arch in great curving trails. The
plant can also be much smaller when it grows in low bushes. It
roots at the tips of its shoots.

Rubus: Lat. name for 'bramble bush.'
Fruticosus: Lat., 'bushy, shrubby.'

GREAT BURNET
Sanguisorba officinalis

Found: Damp places, water meadows. Southern Scotland and England. Rare in Ireland.
Flowers: Summer.
Height: About 2 ft.

Dark red heads of flowers, turning from a round to a more egg or oblong shape, barely 1 in. long. Each head is made up of closely packed little flowers, firm to the touch, and grows at the top of a strong branched stalk. The plant is much larger than *Salad Burnet* (p. 216).

The leaves are attractively cut into pairs of leaflets each on short stalks from the main midrib, and regularly notched, with one central end leaflet. They chiefly grow from the root, or from the lower part of the stem.

Sanguisorba: From Lat. *sanguis*, 'blood,' and *sorbere*, 'to suck up,' from its former use in stanching wounds.

Officinalis: From Lat. *officina*, 'workshop,' because the plant was used by the old herbalists.

SALAD BURNET
Poterium Sanguisorba

Found: Dry places, limestone rocks, chalky places. Common in Britain in limestone districts, scarce in Scotland and Ireland. *Flowers:* Summer. *Height:* About 1 ft.

Rounded flower heads, a greenish red, grow at the end of upright slender stalks. The head has a fringed look, as the lower flowers (male) have long stamens hanging from them. The upper flowers are female and feathery.

The long leaves are cut into about fifteen or more leaflets, which are small, egg-shaped, and toothed, and grow in pairs, each leaflet having its own short stalk, the leaflets getting larger near the top. The leaves have a cucumber flavour and are often used in salads.

The stems are slender and erect, and slightly downy.

Poterium: Lat., 'drinking cup,' because the leaves were used as a flavouring. *Sanguisorba:* From Lat. *sanguis*, 'blood,' and *sorbere*, 'to suck up,' from its former use in staunching wounds.

216

DOG ROSE
Rosa canina

Found: Hedges and thickets. Common in Britain. *Flowers:* Early summer. *Height:* Long trailing branches, 6–8 ft. long.

The delicate flowers with the conspicuous bunch of yellow stamens in the centre are usually sweet-scented. They generally grow singly, but sometimes two or three together. The flowers are easily distinguished from the *Field Rose* (p. 26), which is white and scentless. The fruit is scarlet.

The leaves are stalked and smooth, with toothed edges, and each cut into five egg-shaped, pointed leaflets. There are sharp thorns on the backs of the leaves. Two lobed stipules are joined to the leaf stalks like wings.

The stem is upright when the plant is young, later branches and straggles with sharp hooked thorns upon it.

Rosa: Lat. name, from the Gk. word *rhodon*, 'rose.'
Canina: From Lat. *canis*, 'dog,' meaning that it is a common (or valueless) flower.

217

ROSEBAY WILLOW-HERB
Epilobium angustifolium

Found: Damp woods and clearings. Common throughout Britain.
Flowers: Summer. *Height:* 3–4 ft.

A handsome plant that grows in masses in open woods, especially where trees have recently been cut down, spreading like a weed by means of suckers. The brightly coloured rosy flowers (about 1 in. across) have four petals, almost square when fully open, with a wide gap between two of the petals through which the eight stamens protrude and bend down. The flowers grow in loose showy spikes at the head of the stem. The apparent flower stalk eventually thickens and lengthens to become the seed pod, and ends by splitting; the seeds inside each have long, delicate, silky hairs and float away in the wind.

The leaves are narrowly lance-shaped, and can be as long as 6 in. They grow closely up the stem on very short stalks, giving it an almost bushy appearance, and seem to have a hem round their edges, which are waved and crinkled.

The stem is strong, upright, smooth, reddish, and unbranched.

Epilobium: From Gk. *epi,* 'upon,' and *lobos,* 'a pod,' because the flower is placed closely on top of the seed pod.
Angustifolium: Lat., 'with narrow leaves.'

CODLINS-AND-CREAM
Epilobium hirsutum

Found: Damp places, ditches and low-lying ground. Common in England, less so in Scotland. *Flowers:* Summer. *Height:* 3–4 ft.

Also called the *Great Willow-herb*.

Handsome rose-coloured flowers (about ¾ in. across) are bunched loosely at the head of the tall stem. The flowers are funnel-shaped and then open out, the petals being notched and paling to white in the centre of the flower. What at first sight look like square flower stalks are really seed vessels, and soon thicken into long reddish, narrow, hairy pods. The seeds are eventually carried away by the wind, as they have tufts of long white hairs.

The leaves are lance-shaped with small regular saw-like teeth; they clasp the stem and are very hairy.

The stem is tall and strong, much branched and hairy. The plant grows in masses, and is rather a coarse plant.

Epilobium: From Gk. *epi,* 'upon,' and *lobos,* 'a pod,' because the flower is placed closely on top of the seed pod.

Hirsutum: Lat., 'hairy.'

ENCHANTER'S NIGHTSHADE

Circaea lutetiana

Found: Shady places, damp woods. Common in England and Ireland, less so in Scotland. *Flowers:* Summer. *Height:* 1–1½ ft.

Spikes of pale pink little flowers (⅛ in. across) are set rather far apart, each on a tiny stalk of its own, and enclosed in a minute hairy calyx. Each flower has only two deeply notched petals, with pinkish hairs inside. The little egg-shaped fruits have hooked bristles, and by the time they develop the flower stalk turns downwards.

The leaves grow opposite each other and are stalked, egg-shaped and pointed, about 2–3 in. long, and smooth. They are clearly veined and the veins which run up the sides of the leaf do so in loops along the edges.

The stalk is slender, square and tall, covered with whitish hairs.

Circaea: After Circe, the enchantress, because the fruit with its hooked prickles lays hold of passers-by, as in the ancient fable Circe laid hold of men with her enchantments.

Lutetiana: Lat., 'native to Lutetia,' the Roman name for Paris.

PURPLE LOOSESTRIFE
Lythrum Salicaria

Found: Banks of streams, ditches, wet places. Common in England, Ireland, and southern and western Scotland.
Flowers: Summer. *Height:* 3–5 ft.

The flowers make a handsome spike as they grow in rings at the head of the stem, each about $\frac{1}{2}$ in. across. Each flower has a tubular calyx with twelve teeth, and has four to six oblong petals and twice as many stamens. Leafy green bracts grow up the stem amongst the flowers. The plant grows in masses.

The leaves are lance-shaped, and grow in pairs or in rings, stalkless, and clasping the stem, with plain edges.

The stem is hard and angled and sometimes winged. It is very erect.

Lythrum: From Gk. *luthron*, 'gore,' from the purple colour of the flowers.

Salicaria: From Lat. *salix*, 'willow,' because of the shape of the leaves.

HONEYSUCKLE
Lonicera Periclymenum

Found: Hedges, thickets, woods.   Common in Britain.   *Flowers:* Summer and autumn.   *Height:* Climbs and twines to great lengths.

Sweetly scented flowers, in shades varying from white to red, pink, and yellow (they become yellow after pollination), grow in large clusters at the head of the stem.   The flowers are in crowded heads, each with a green calyx of five teeth.   The long flower tube divides to form an open mouth, from which the stamens and long style stick out.   The flowers are very rich in nectar; after they have withered round scarlet berries form, bunched together.

The egg-shaped leaves grow in pairs, the upper ones stalkless. They are smooth and shining above, downy underneath, with plain edges.

The stem is tough and may be rather woody.   It twines to a length of 10 to 20 ft., and always from left to right.

Lonicera: After Adam Lonicer, a Frankfort botanist of the sixteenth century.
Periclymenum: Gk. name for Honeysuckle.

FIELD MADDER

Sherardia arvensis

Found: Common as a weed of cultivated ground, also in waste places in greater part of Britain, but scarce in northern Scotland. *Flowers:* The whole summer. *Height:* Up to 6 in.

The small flowers grow in clustered heads at the top of the stem. closely surrounded with a leafy involucre which is deeply cut into about eight lobes, which are longer than the flowers themselves. The latter are tubular each opening into four spreading petals.

The small leaves usually grow in rings of six up the stem, the lower leaves oval, the upper ones more lance-shaped. They are roughly edged and taper to a fine point.

The stem branches from the base, and spreads on the ground.

Sherardia: Named after William Sherard, a botanist born in 1659.
Arvensis: Lat., 'of the fields.'

WILD TEASEL
Dipsacus fullonum

Found: Roadsides, waste places, copse-sides, woods.　Common in southern England, less so in the north.　*Flowers:* Late summer.　*Height:* 3–5 ft.

A conspicuous tall plant with thistle-like, prickly, cone-shaped heads (3 in. long and 1½ in. across).　Round this are eight to twelve strong spines (bracts), some longer than the head itself, and which curve up above it, ending in fine sharp points.　These spines have prickles down the centre and on the outside.

The root-leaves are stalked, lance-shaped and very prickly, and lie in a prickly rosette on the ground, about 18 in. across.　They die after the first year.　The stem leaves grow in pairs and are stalkless; the lower leaves join together and so form a cup that holds dew and rain. The plant can endure long periods of drought.

The stem is stout, angular, prickly, and rigidly upright.

Dipsacus: From Gk. *dipsakos*, 'teasel,' from *dipsa*, 'thirst,' because the leaves unite and hold water to satisfy thirst.
Fullonum: Lat., 'of fullers,' a variety of the plant being used by fullers to tease out cloth.

HEMP AGRIMONY
Eupatorium cannabinum

Found: Damp places, banks of streams. Throughout Britain. *Flowers:* Summer and autumn. *Height:* 3–4 ft.

The plant usually grows in leafy masses, the flower heads in thick clusters at the head of tall stems. These have a ragged feathery look (fading to grey late in the summer) as the tubular little flowers have long branched styles sticking out like threads. The flowers have a sweet scent.

The leaves are usually divided into three parts, lance-shaped, slightly downy, and coarsely toothed, 2–4 in. long.

The stem is coarse, downy and tall, hard, woody and reddish, and stands erect.

Eupatorium: The classical name of the plant after Mithradates Eupator, King of Pontus, who was said to have discovered its use in medicine.

Cannabinum: Lat., 'hemp-like,' from *kannabis*, the Gk. name for the hemp plant, which it is supposed to resemble.

225

BLUE FLEABANE

Erigeron acer

Found: Dry places, fields, banks, chalk downs. Not very common in England and Ireland. Rare in Scotland. *Flowers:* Late summer and autumn. *Height:* 6 in.–1 ft.

Small flower-heads (not blue, but a pinkish mauve) ½ in. across, the centre florets pale yellow. They do not open out flat like so many of the Daisy Family, but are encased in a small bristly cup or calyx, tinged with red, and turn into fluffy seed-bearing heads. The flower-heads grow singly on long stalks, which branch to give the effect of a very loose cluster.

The root leaves are broadly lance-shaped, with plain untoothed edges. They wither early. The stem leaves are very narrow, and get smaller the higher up the stem they are, and half clasp it.

The stem is upright and slender, hairy, and varies much in height. It often tends to be reddish in colour.

Erigeron: From Gk. *ēri,* 'early,' and *gerōn,* 'old,' because the heads of flowers turn into a fluffy greyness, like the grey head of an old man. *Acer:* Lat. 'sharp,' because of the bitter taste of the plant.

226

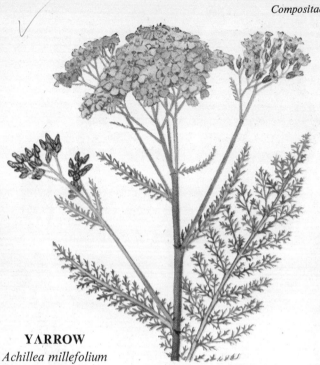

YARROW
Achillea millefolium

Found: Waste ground, fields, and roadsides.   Very common in Britain.
Flowers: The whole summer.   *Height:* 1 ft.

Sometimes called *Milfoil*.   The crowded heads of small pink flowers are often white (p. 47).   They grow together at the top of the branched stems in flat heads, unlike most other flowers in this family.

The leaves are so cut and divided as to give the plant a feathery appearance, and they mostly spring from the root.

The stem is strong and upright, a greenish-grey colour and ridged, and covered with soft woolly hairs.

The plant is usually very hairy, but can be found quite smooth.

Achillea: Named after Achilles, who is supposed to have been the first to discover the healing virtues of the plant.

Millefolium: Lat., 'bearing a thousand leaves.'

227

BUTTERBUR
Petasites officinalis

Found: Damp banks of streams or roadsides. Common in England and Ireland and southern Scotland. *Flowers:* Early spring. *Height:* 6 in.–1 ft.

Do not confuse with *Winter Heliotrope*, which does not really rank as a wild flower and is smaller and very sweetly scented.

The *Butterbur* comes into flower before its leaves are open, the flesh-coloured heads of flowers grouped together in a long, close, club-shaped spike at the head of the stem.

The leaves are more or less heart-shaped, toothed, and can be as large as 3 ft. across. They have white cobwebby hairs, more particularly underneath, when young, and grow on long stalks. They are deeply wrinkled and have pinkish veins. The stem is stout and fleshy.

Petasites: From Gk. *petasos*, 'a broad-brimmed hat,' because of the dense shade afforded by the large leaves.
Officinalis: From Lat. *officina*, 'workshop,' because the plant was used by the old herbalists.

228

COMMON BURDOCK
Arctium vulgare

Found: Waste places, roadsides.   Common in Britain.   *Flowers:* Summer.
Height: 3–4 ft.

A coarse bushy plant.   Purple thistle-like heads crowd together in
the leaf axils at the head of the stem.   The rounded involucre con-
sists of leathery scales (bracts), each having a long sharp hook.   The
heads, when ripened and full of seeds, catch in anything that may
come in touch with them (the fur of animals, the clothes of passers-by),
and are carried away.   The name 'bur-dock' is thus very appropriate.

The root leaves are very large, thick, and heart-shaped.   They may
be 18 in. long and 12 in. broad.   Underneath they are covered with a
white cottony down, and have waved edges and a crinkled look.
The stem leaves are much smaller, and are broadly oval.

The stem is stout, erect, and branching.

Arctium: From the Gk. *arktos,* 'bear,' because of the rough bristly feel
of the flower heads.
Vulgare: Lat., 'common.'

SPEAR THISTLE
Carduus lanceolatus

Found: Waste ground, fields, commons. Throughout Britain. *Flowers:* Summer and early autumn. *Height:* 3–4 ft.

A very common plant with purple flower heads, which emerge from the prickly involucres like soft rounded plumes. They grow at the head of short stalks, sometimes solitary but usually three in a cluster. They are about 1¾ in. long when fully out.

The head itself is made up of numerous tiny tubular flowers, and the involucre is cone-shaped and large, each small scale (bract) ending in a hard sharp prickle. The flowers are followed by plumes of silky down, blown away by the wind, dispersing the seeds which they carry.

The leaves are lance-shaped but cut into narrow lobes, the end one much the longest. Each lobe ends in a stiff prickle, and is usually cut again into two divisions stiffly spined. The upper side of the leaf has short stiff bristly hairs, the underside is white and cottony. The leaves vary in length, but can be a foot long.

The stem is very upright, stout, and grooved, and has sharply prickled wings down it.

Carduus: Lat. name for 'thistle.'
Lanceolatus: Lat., 'like a spear-head,' because of the shape of the leaves.

230

CREEPING THISTLE

Carduus arvensis

Found: Cultivated and waste places. Common in Britain. *Flowers:* Summer. *Height:* 2–4 ft.

A common farmland weed, the flowers grow in loose clusters at the head of branched stems and are not large. The involucre is made up of rows of small spiny bracts.

The leaves are stalkless and embrace the stem, lance-shaped but deeply cut, with prickly edges, and each with a long sharp spine at its tip.

The stem is erect, branched, leafy, ribbed, with the prickles of the leaves continuing on the stem where they join it.

Carduus: Lat. name for 'thistle.'
Arvensis: Lat., 'of the fields.'

231

WOOLLY-HEADED THISTLE
Carduus eriophorus

Found: Waste places, chalk and limestone districts of southern England. Some parts of Yorkshire. Not common. *Flowers:* Summer. *Height:* 4–6ft.

The most handsome of all the thistles, with large purple flower-heads (about 2½ in. across) looking rather like a flattened shaving brush. The head is covered with white cobwebby wool, through which the overlapping spines stick out their sharp points. Underneath the head are long, slender, needle-pointed green bracts, like a collar or ruff, and covered with bristles. The flowers wither into feathery seed-bearing heads.

The leaves are deeply divided, each lobe ending in a sharp stiff prickle. They are dark green on the upper side, underneath much paler, and coated with a soft cottony down.

The stem is very stout, upright, furrowed, woolly, and branched.

Carduus: Lat. name for 'thistle.'
Eriophorus: From the Gk. *erion*, 'wool,' and *pherein*, 'to bear': 'wool bearer.'

BLACK KNAPWEED
Centaurea nigra

Found: Fields and meadows, grassy roadsides, dry places.   Common in Britain.   *Flowers:* All the summer.   *Height:* 1–2 ft.

Compare with the more feathery-looking and larger *Great Knapweed* (p. 234).

A tall plant with thistle-like heads (about 1 in. across) at the ends of branched stems.   The heads are rounded and made up of tiny tubular flowers, those of the outer rings being sometimes larger than the inner. Small tight scales (bracts) form the involucre, overlapping in close rows edged and fringed with brown.

The leaves are narrow, rough, lance-shaped, and those on the stem stalkless.

The stem is hard, tough, ribbed, and slightly branched.

Centaurea: One of the plants said to have been discovered by the centaur Chiron.

Nigra: Lat., 'black.'

233

GREAT KNAPWEED
Centaurea Scabiosa

Found: Fields, waste and chalky places, waysides. Fairly common in England, less so in Scotland, rare in Ireland. *Flowers:* Summer and autumn. *Height:* 2–3 ft.

An altogether stouter plant than the *Black Knapweed* (p. 233) and with differently shaped leaves.

The outer ring of tiny tubular flowers of the large head have a handsome fringed effect, each flower cut into five long narrow lobes. Below is the hard rounded involucre of small triangular scales (bracts) which are green, edged with black, with a bristly black fringe.

The leaves are large and deeply cut into notched lobes irregularly spaced apart. Near the top of the stem the leaves are smaller and simpler.

The stem is grooved, hard and hairy, erect and branched.

Centaurea: One of the plants said to have been discovered by the centaur Chiron.
Scabiosa: Lat., 'rough,' 'scurfy,' from *scabies*, 'the itch.'

COMMON HEATH
Erica cinerea

Found: Moorlands, dry heaths. Throughout Britain. *Flowers:* Summer and autumn. *Height:* 6 in.–18 in

Sometimes called *Bell Heather*, this well-known Heath grows over large tracts of land, and covers hills, moors, and cliff sides with its purple flowers.

These grow in dense spikes ringed round the main stem on short stalks, and are bell- or egg-shaped, about $\frac{1}{4}$ in. long, cut into four small teeth at the mouth.

The leaves are almost needle-like and very finely pointed, growing in rings of three, with clusters of short leaves in their axils, giving the stalk a tufted look.

The plant is bushy and the stem woody and shrublike, branching from the base. It lies on the ground and straggles, the branches growing upright, and is tough, wiry, and reddish.

Erica: From Gk. *ereikē,* 'heath' or 'heather.'
Cinerea: Lat., 'ash-coloured.'

CROSS-LEAVED HEATH

Erica Tetralix

Found: Moors, commons, damp boggy places, woods. Common in Britain. *Flowers:* Late summer. *Height:* 6–18 in.

Distinguished from the *Common Heath* (p. 235) by the way the pale rose-coloured flowers grow in drooping bunches or clusters at the head of the stem. They are egg-shaped, the mouth of the flower cut into four tiny parts.

The needle-like leaves grow up the stem in rings of four, and are hairy with fringed edges.

The stem is slender and wiry, branched and downy.

Erica: From Gk. *ereikē,* 'heath' or 'heather.'

Tetralix: Gk. name for 'heath,' *tetra,* 'four,' referring to the arrangement of the leaves.

236

HEATHER or LING
Calluna vulgaris

Found: Heaths and moors. Common throughout Britain. *Flowers:* Summer. *Height:* 6 in.–2 ft.

Sometimes called *Scottish Heather*, and the commonest of all the Heaths. This is the heather from which honey comes, bee-keepers often taking their hives to the moors at the time of the nectar flow.

The flowers are tiny, satiny and bell-shaped, and grow in loose leafy spikes, tending to bleach white as they grow older. They are each deeply split into four, the petals inside the outer bell of pointed pink sepals. The plant is really a low, straggling, and much-branched shrub.

The leaves are very narrow, with edges curled underneath, like small hard spines overlapping each other on the stem.

The stem is tough, woody and wiry, and a reddish colour; much branched.

Calluna: From the Gk. *kallunein,* 'to sweep,' because the twigs of the plant were made into brooms.
Vulgaris: Lat., 'common.'

237

SCARLET PIMPERNEL
Anagallis arvensis

Found: Waste places, cultivated ground.   Common in Britain.   *Flowers:* The whole season.   *Height:* 6 in.–1 ft.

A common garden weed.   Each flower springs singly on a slender little stalk from the leaf axil.   It is encased in a green calyx of narrow sharply pointed sepals, almost as long as the petals.   The flowers close at the threat of rain, and are sometimes blue.

The leaves are stalkless, smooth, oval and pointed, with plain edges, and grow in pairs.

The tough main stem lies on the ground, and sends up short smooth stalks.

Anagallis: Gk. name for 'pimpernel.

Arvensis: Lat., 'of the fields.'

BOG PIMPERNEL

Anagallis tenella

Found: Bogs and banks of streams, wet places. Greater part of Britain, more especially in the west and in Ireland. *Flowers:* Summer. *Height:* Creeping.

A creeping plant, very delicate and slender. The flowers grow upwards on thread-like stalks, and are narrowly bell-shaped, very delicate, and cleft into five. The calyx is small. The stamens have woolly stalks.

The little egg-shaped leaves grow opposite each other, with very short stalks.

The stem lies on the ground, creeping and rooting in damp earth. It is very slender and branched, 3–4 in. long. The flower stalks rise from it.

Anagallis: Gk. name for 'pimpernel.'

Tenella: Lat., 'somewhat tender and delicate.'

239

COMMON CENTAURY
Erythraea Centaurium

Found: Sandy fields, dry places, roadsides.   Common in Britain.   *Flowers:*
All the summer.   *Height:* 3 in.–1 ft.

The flowers grow in clusters on freely forking stems at the head of
the main stem; they tend to close early in the day and in damp weather.
They open out into five star-like, clean-cut petals. This is a neat,
trim plant.

The stem leaves are smooth and stalkless; they grow in pairs, joined
together, but each pair spaced widely apart. The root leaves are
oval and form a spreading tuft or rosette.

The stem is very erect, slender, and square, and much forked at
the top.

Erythraea: From Gk. *eruthraios*, 'reddish.'
Centaurium: One of the plants said to have been discovered by the centaur
Chiron.

240

FELWORT
Gentiana Amarella

Found: Dry fields, chalk downs. Over the greater part of Britain
Flowers: End of summer and autumn. *Height:* 4 in.–1 ft.

One of the British gentians.

Pinkish purple tubular flowers grow in loose or in crowded, leafy,
spike-like clusters, each on a short stalk springing from the main
stem. The flower tube opens out into five pointed petals. The calyx
is tubular, and the five sepals are joined together, deeply divided into
five sharp points. Fine hairs grow in the mouth of the flower. The
plant often has a purplish tinge.

The leaves grow in pairs and clasp the stem; they are lance-shaped.
The root leaves are broader and more oval.

The stem is very erect, branched, leafy, and reddish.

Gentiana: After Gentius, a king of Illyria, who is said to have discovered
healing qualities in this plant.
Amarella: Lat., 'bitter,' literally 'the little bitter one.'

241

SMALL BINDWEED
Convolvulus arvensis

Found: Fields, waste places, hedges. Common in England and Ireland, local in Scotland. *Flowers:* All the summer. *Height:* Creeps, trails, and twines to about 2 ft. lengths.

Small trumpet-shaped flowers (about 1 in. across), with five petals joined to form a widely open funnel. The sepals, of a darker pink and narrowly pointed, seem to lie on the back of the flower. The flowers are scented, and close at night or in bad weather.

The leaves are arrow-shaped, stalked, and very smooth, about 1½ in. long, with spreading, pointed, ear-like bases.

The stem is slender and twines round grass stems or corn stalks and over hedges. But more often the plant is prostrate.

Convolvulus: From Lat. *convolvere,* 'to twine.'
Arvensis: Lat., 'of the fields.'

COMFREY
Symphytum officinale

Found: Ditches, shady and wet places. Fairly common in England and Ireland, less so in Scotland. *Flowers:* Spring and summer. *Height:* 2 ft.–3 ft.

The flowers are often a creamy white (p. 49). Usually a rather coarse, tall, heavy plant, covered with hairy bristles. The flowers are bell-shaped. They droop in one-sided spikes, each little tubular flower pinched in at the end as if by a finger-nail.

The leaves are large, coarse, bristly, sometimes nearly a foot long. They run down the stem as if it were winged on each side; the lower leaves are stalked. They have an aromatic smell, and can be used for flavouring in cooking.

The stem is thick and soft, deeply grooved, and very hairy.

Symphytum: From Gk. *sumphuein*, 'to unite,' because the plant was formerly thought to be helpful in healing wounds.

Officinale: From Lat. *officina*, 'workshop,' because the plant was used by the old herbalists.

243

HOUND'S-TONGUE
Cynoglossum officinale

Found: Waste places, waysides. Fairly common in England and southern
Scotland, but only in south-east of Ireland. *Flowers:* Summer. *Height:*
About 2 ft.

A rather coarse plant that has a greyish look because it is covered
with soft hairs. The flowers (nearly ½ in. across) grow in clusters
on forked stems and are a curious maroon colour, encased in a grey-
green calyx, and tend to close as soon as picked. When they wither
there are four flat nutlets covered with hooked bristles.

The lower leaves are stalked and up to a foot long, broadly lance-
shaped. The upper leaves are stalkless and clasp the stem. They
are covered with downy hairs, and have waved edges.

The stem is stout, upright and branched, and is covered with hairs.
The plant has an unpleasant mousy smell.

Cynoglossum: From Gk. *kuōn*, 'dog,' and *glōssa*, 'tongue.'
Officinale: From Lat. *officina*, 'workshop,' because the plant was used
by the old herbalists.

244

HENBANE
Hyoscyamus niger

Found: Waste and stony places. Rubbish heaps and near old walls. Not particularly common in England, southern Scotland, and Ireland. *Flowers:* Summer. *Height:* 1–2 ft.

This is really a dingy yellow flower, but it is usually so covered with fine purple veins that the effect is a dull purplish red. The flowers grow in one-sided spikes amongst leaves at the head of the stem; they are very shortly stalked when they are in the forks of the branches, but without stalks nearer the top. The flower is about 1 in. long, and widely bell-shaped.

The leaves from the root are large and oval, 7–8 in. long. The stem leaves are stalkless, and clasp the stem. They are cut into angular lobes, which are covered with sticky hairs. The whole plant is hairy and rather sticky and has an unpleasant smell.

The stem is stout, branching, round, and hairy. The plant is poisonous, and was much used in the old days as a drug. From it comes the valuable drug hyoscine.

Hyoscyamus: From *huoskuamos,* 'hog-bean,' the Gk. name for the plant. *Niger:* Lat., 'black.'

BITTERSWEET or WOODY NIGHTSHADE

Solanum Dulcamara

Found: Hedgerows and thickets. Throughout England and Ireland, less common in Scotland. *Flowers:* Summer. *Height:* Trails and climbs to lengths of 4–5 ft.

This plant has no actual means of climbing or twining, but manages to support itself on other hedgerow bushes.

The flowers have five pointed petals in the centre of which the conspicuous bright yellow anthers (the pollen-bearing tips of the stamens) stick out, cone-shaped, while the petals bend back and away from them. At the base of each petal are two small 'tubercles' which together make a green ring round the centre of the flower. The fruit, which is unwholesome, changes from a green berry to yellow, then orange, and finally scarlet.

The leaves vary, the lower ones being heart-shaped, very often with two ear-shaped lobes at their base, and all are stalked. They are smooth, with plain edges.

The stem is long and trailing, much branched, rather woody at the foot but weaker above.

Solanum: The Lat. name of the plant.
Dulcamara: From Lat. *dulcis,* 'sweet,' and *amarus,* 'bitter.'

246

DEADLY
NIGHTSHADE
Atropa Belladonna

Found: Stony waste places, near ruins and old walls, chalky wastes. Rather rare. Southern England and certain localities in the north. *Flowers:* Summer. *Height:* 3–4 ft.

A purplish bell-shaped flower (about 1 in. long), the mouth cut into five divisions. It droops and grows singly on short stalks springing from the axil of the leaves and the main stem. The berry is large, shining and black, and very poisonous. The plant has an unpleasant smell and is also poisonous, though the juice is used in modern medicine.

The leaves are large with short stalks, and grow in pairs, one being much smaller than the other, and covered with fine hairs.

The stem is upright and stout, branching like a bush.

Atropa: From the Gk. Atropos, one of the Fates.

Belladonna: Modern Lat. from Ital. for 'beautiful lady,' because of use made of the plant for enlarging the pupils of the eyes, thereby making them brighter.

CREEPING TOADFLAX

Linaria repens

Found: Stony places, waste ground.   Rare in Britain.   *Flowers:* Summer and autumn.   *Height:* 8 in.–2 ft.

The flowers are almost white, but the purple and bluish veins of the petals produce a lilac effect.   They have little spurs, and grow in short spikes or clusters at the head of the stem.

The leaves are crowded together in rings at the foot of the stem, and also grow more sparsely at its upper end.

The stems lie on the ground at the base.

Linaria: From Lat. *linum,* 'flax,' because the leaves of some plants of this group resemble those of Flax.

Repens: Lat., 'creeping.'

IVY-LEAVED TOADFLAX
Linaria Cymbalaria

Found: Old walls, ruins, stony places. Common in England and southern Scotland. *Flowers:* The whole season. *Height:* Spreads and trails from 6 in. to 2 ft.

Tiny lilac flowers grow singly on very slender stalks. Each flower has two lips and a short spur. The under lip is a deeper lilac streaked with two purple lines, the upper one is rounded, and what is called the palate closes the tube and is yellow, so attracting insects to the opening and the concealed honey. After the seed has formed the little flower stalk bends towards the stone or crack in the wall in which the seed may grow.

The leaves are ivy-shaped, with long reddish thin stalks. They tend to be tinged with purple underneath. They are rather thick and very smooth, more shining below than above.

The stems are very slender and reddish, often rooting at the axils of the leaf stalks. They are much branched and trailing.

Linaria: From Lat. *linum*, 'flax,' because the leaves of some plants in this group resemble those of Flax.

Cymbalaria: Lat. name for some plant.

249

KNOTTED FIGWORT

Scrophularia nodosa

Found: Shady damp places, undergrowth, waste ground. All over Britain. *Flowers:* Summer and autumn. *Height:* 2–3 ft.

Compare with *Water Figwort* (see next page). It has similar curious little flowers, in this case growing in loose very open stalked clusters up the stem. The dark red lip stands up over the little green goblet-shaped flower, with its open mouth; the lowest lip spreads outwards.

The leaves grow in pairs, are broadly egg-shaped and pointed, stalked shortly up the stem, and about 2–4 in. long. They are usually doubly toothed, more deeply so at the base. They thin out at the top of the stem to none at all.

The stem is tall and straight, square, sometimes a dark red on the exposed side. It is thick and strong. There is a purplish line down the leaf stalk and partly up the mid-rib. The plant has an unpleasant smell when crushed.

Scrophularia: From Lat. *scrofula*, a disease for which the plant was considered a remedy. *Nodosa:* Lat., 'knotted,' because of the swollen roots.

WATER FIGWORT
Scrophularia aquatica

Found: Ditches, marshes, banks of streams. Common in England.
Flowers: Summer.   *Height:* 1–3 ft., but may grow much taller.

Compare with *Knotted Figwort*.

Curious little goblet-shaped flowers each with an upright lip, like the pricked ear of a mouse. They grow in long clusters and are a red-brown colour on the upper side, and a paler green below. The flowers can also be white.

The leaves are stalked, narrowly oval, and evenly toothed. They do not grow from the upper part of the stalk.

The stem is strong, stout and square, deeply grooved and reddish. Near the foot narrow leafy wings grow out from the angles of the stem.

Scrophularia: From Lat. *scrofula*, a disease for which the plant was considered a remedy.

Aquatica: Lat., 'found in or by water.'

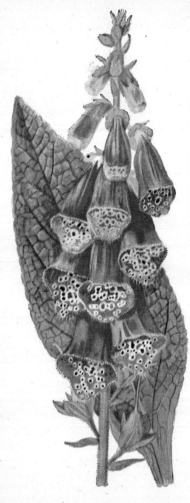

FOXGLOVE
Digitalis purpurea

Found: Roadsides, dry banks, cliffs, woodlands. Common in Britain. *Flowers:* Spring and summer. *Height:* 2–4 ft.

The large bell-shaped flowers grow in tall spikes and all droop on the same side of the stem; they are about 1–1½ in. long, and could fit over a small finger. They can be white, and are speckled with purple inside. The lowest of the four lobes of each flower is longer than the others and hairy inside.

The first year the leaves lie on the ground in a rosette, and the second year the tall stem springs up. The root leaves grow on long stalks and are 6 in. long or more, pointed, wrinkled, soft, and downy, smooth above and hairy underneath, with a network of ribs under the larger leaves which stand out in relief.

The stem is downy and strong and very upright.

Digitalis: Lat., 'belonging to the finger.'
Purpurea: Lat., 'purple.'

RED BARTSIA

Bartsia Odontites

Found: Fields, waste places, cornfields. Throughout Britain. *Flowers:* Summer. *Height:* 8 in.–1 ft.

The little tubular flowers, with a long upper lip, are bunched together in one-sided leafy spikes. The plant is shrub-like and bushy.

The stalkless leaves are narrow, lance-shaped and toothed, and grow opposite each other.

The stems are wiry, hard and hairy, tinged with red and branched.

Bartsia: Named after Johann Bartsch, a German botanist.

Odontites: From Gk. *odous,* 'tooth,' as the plant was supposed to cure the toothache.

EYEBRIGHT

Euphrasia officinalis

Found: Fields and commons. Common in Britain. *Flowers:* Summer and autumn. *Height:* 2–6 in.

A lowly plant, much branched, and varying in size. The flowers are white, streaked with purple, so that the effect is pink or pinkish mauve, the centre of the lower lip being yellow. They grow in loose leafy spikes at the end of the branched stems.

The leaves are small and have no stalks. They are a dark green and grow thickly up the stem in pairs, and are deeply toothed.

The stem is stiff and erect.

Euphraśia: Gk., 'delight.'
Officinalis: From Lat. *officina*, 'workshop,' because the plant was used by the old herbalists.

GIPSY-WORT

Lycopus europaeus

Found: Damp places, near ditches and ponds and marshes. Common in England and Ireland, less so in the north. *Flowers:* Summer. *Height:* 3 ft.

Small bell-shaped stalkless flowers grow in close rings on the main stem at the axils of each pair of leaves. They are a pinkish colour, dotted with purple, the calyx cut into five stiffly pointed teeth.

The leaves grow in pairs and have sharply cut edges, narrowly oval, with very short stalks.

The stem is square and erect, and slightly hairy.

Lycopus: From Gk. *lukos,* 'a wolf,' and *pous,* 'foot,' from a fancied resemblance of the leaves.

Europaeus: Lat., 'European.'

255

HORSE MINT
Mentha longifolia

Found: Wet fields, ditches, waste places. Rare in northern counties of Britain. *Flowers:* Late summer. *Height:* 1–2 ft.

The flowers grow in dense spikes (1–2 in. long). Usually several of these are bunched together at the head of the stem. The protruding stamens give the spikes a fringed effect.

The leaves are stalkless, broadly lance-shaped but narrowing near the top of the stem. They are toothed and rather grey, because of the white hairs with which they are covered, more so underneath.

The stem is square and covered with white woolly hairs. The plant has a strong smell of peppermint.

Mentha: Lat. name for 'mint.'

Longifolia: Lat., 'having long leaves,' from *longus*, 'long,' and *folium*, 'leaf.'

WILD THYME
Thymus Serpyllum

Found: Dry hill fields, heath lands, downs. Common in Britain. *Flowers:*
The whole summer. *Height:* 3 in.–1 ft.

The tiny flowers—pink or mauve—grow in rings so closely together
as to look like loose leafy spikes. The whole plant is covered with
hairs. The flowers have a lovely aromatic scent, and are rich in
nectar, so are much frequented by bees.

The leaves are small and egg-shaped, with very short stalks, and
have several long hairs at their bases.

The stem creeps along the ground, sending up the flowering stalks.
It is hard, and the plant grows like a carpet.

Thymus: From Gk. *thumos*, connected with *thuein*, 'to sacrifice,' because
in ancient times the plant was used as incense in the temples.

Serpyllum. From *herpullon*, Gk. name of the plant, from *herpein*, 'to
creep.'

WILD MARJORAM
Origanum vulgare

Found: Banks, roadsides, chalky districts. Spread over England and Ireland, rarer in Scotland. *Flowers:* Summer. *Height:* 1–2 ft.

The small flowers are crowded together in loosely rounded heads at the ends of branched stems; the effect is that of a clustered spike of blossom. The stamens stick out of the mouths of the flowers giving a ragged look. The flowers have a sweet aromatic scent.

The leaves are stalked and grow in pairs, oval and pointed and downy, usually with plain edges.

The stems are erect and hairy.

Origanum: From Gk. *origanon*, probably from *oros*, 'mountain,' and *ganos*, 'beauty.'

Vulgare: Lat., 'common.'

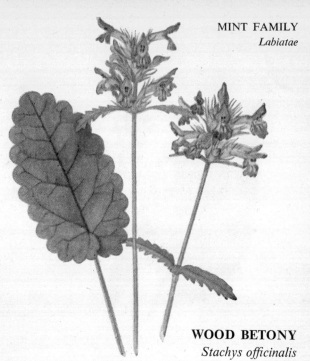

WOOD BETONY
Stachys officinalis

Found: Woods, thickets, hedge banks, grassy places.   Common in England, rare in Scotland.   *Flowers:* Summer.   *Height:* 1–2 ft.

The flowers grow in dense rings in an oblong head or spike at the head of the stem, which is almost leafless.   They are tubular, with wide-open mouths, and hairy, the tube being much longer than the calyx with its sharply pointed teeth.   The upper lip stands erect and hood-like, the lower is spread out and broad.   Two long, narrow, green bracts grow at the bottom of the spike of flowers, and usually hang down, and smaller bracts below each calyx.

The leaves are hairy and mostly grow from the root.   They are roundly oblong, on long stalks, with rounded teeth.   The upper leaves are few, stalkless or with very short stalks, quite narrow and sharply toothed, and a distinctive pair of small leaves grows at right angles to the stem.

The stem is square and hairy.

Stachys: From Gk. *stachus,* 'a spike.'
Officinalis: From Lat. *officina,* 'workshop,' because the plant was used by the old herbalists.

HEDGE WOUNDWORT
Stachys sylvatica

Found: Edges of woods, in shady places at the foot of banks, in thick vegetation. Common in Britain. *Flowers:* Summer. *Height:* 2–4 ft.

The flowers grow in rings on the upper part of the stem, usually in sixes, and more crowded together at the top, so that the effect is of a flowering spike. They are tubular with two lips, the upper one like a hood, the lower marked with white and hanging down. The calyx has five pointed teeth, but the tube of the flower is the longer of the two.

The leaves are large, heart-shaped, soft to the touch, and closely covered with soft bristly hairs, specially above. They are about 2½ in. long, and toothed, and something like the *Stinging-nettle* leaves to look at. They are stalked and grow in pairs, getting smaller up the stem.

The stem is hairy, rough, solid and square, with purple angles. It has an unpleasant smell.

Stachys: From Gk. *stachus,* 'a spike.'
Sylvatica: Lat., 'of the woods.'

BLACK HOREHOUND
Ballota nigra

Found: Roadsides, waste places, under hedges. Common in England, Ireland, and southern Scotland. *Flowers:* Summer and early autumn. *Height:* 2–3 ft.

This plant is very like the *Hedge Woundwort* (p. 260) and the *Dead-nettles* (pp. 51 and 262).

The flowers grow in dense clusters in the leaf axils and are tubular, with one upright arched lip, and a flat lower lip cut into three. They tend to turn to one side. The tubular calyx is long, with prominent ribs and five finely pointed teeth. The petals soon fall, and leave the reddish-brown calyx.

The leaves are grey-green, stalked, wrinkled, hairy and toothed, and grow in pairs. They turn a dark reddish brown as they grow older. The lower leaves are more or less heart-shaped, but more oval higher up the stem.

The stem is stout, square, dark red, and hairy. The plant has an unpleasant smell, and tends to grow in masses.

Ballota: From *ballote*, the Gk. name of the plant.
Nigra: Lat., 'black.'

RED DEAD-NETTLE
Lamium purpureum

Found: Waysides, hedgebanks, and cultivated places.   Common n Britain.
Flowers: The whole season.   *Height:* 6 in. or more.

A common garden weed, as well as growing profusely in grassy
places.   It is very often tinged with dull red, or purple all over.   It is
no relation to the *Stinging-nettle*, though the leaves are something
like each other, and the plants often grow together.

The tubular little flowers are bunched together at the top of the
stalk, and grow in rings just above the leaves, and almost hidden by
them.   Each flower opens into a mouth with a lower lip that sticks
out and is notched, and an upper lip that is hairy and hood-like.

The leaves are heart-shaped, wrinkled, toothed, the lower leaves on
long stalks, the upper smaller and with shorter stalks.

The stem is square and hollow.

Lamium: Lat. for Dead-nettle, from the same Gk. stem as *lamia*, 'a
monster,' referring to the odd appearance of the flower.
Purpureum: Lat., 'purple.'

THRIFT
Armeria maritima

Found: Rocks, cliffs, sea shores, coastal and hilly places. Common in Britain. *Flowers:* Summer. *Height:* 3–8 in.

Often called *Sea Pink.*

Tiny flowers are grouped closely together to form a single rounded head at the top of the stalk, with an involucre (ring of bracts) of small tough scales. The lowest of these grow downwards and form a small reddish sheath round the stalk. The buds are silvery.

The leaves grow in a tuft from the root, and are very narrow. There are no stem leaves.

The flower stems rise from the cushion of leaves, and are softly downy or smooth.

Armeria: Said to be from the Celtic *ar mor,* 'by the sea.'
Maritima: Lat., 'belonging to the sea.'

263

DOCK FAMILY
Polygonaceae

COMMON SORREL
Rumex Acetosa

Found: Fields, waysides. All over Britain. *Flowers:* Summer. *Height:* 1–2 ft.

The small reddish-green flowers grow in loose rings to form spikes along slender branched leafless stems.

The stem leaves are stalkless and clasp it with their arrow-shaped bases; they are long, narrow to a point, and are rather fleshy. The root leaves are also arrow-shaped, with long stalks, and grow in a rosette.

The stem is upright and slender, and tinged with red.

Rumex: Lat. name of the plant.
Acetosa: Lat., 'sour,' from *acetum*, 'vinegar.'

PALE PERSICARIA
Polygonum lapathifolium

Found: Waste ground, cornfields, and cultivated ground. Fairly common in Britain, less so in the north. *Flowers:* Summer and early autumn. *Height:* 1–2 ft., inclined to lie and spread on the ground.

A garden weed. Small pinkish-green flowers with red tips grow in close inch-long spikes, tightly like grains. The whole effect is pink, hard, and tight.

The leaves usually have a distinctive black marking, like a small blotch, and are broadly lance-shaped.

The stem is smooth, swollen at the joints, and brittle. It lies on the ground and spreads and roots widely, and also rises erect. It is often a reddish colour.

Polygonum: From Gk. *polus,* 'many,' and *gonu,* 'a joint,' because of the numerous joints or knots in the stems.

Lapathifolium: Lat., 'having leaves like those of sorrel.'

265

EARLY PURPLE ORCHIS
Orchis mascula

Found: Fields, woodlands, damp and shady places. One of the commonest of the wild orchids and found all over Britain. *Flowers:* Spring and early summer. *Height:* 12–18 in.

The flowers vary from bright purple or purplish-pink to pale pink, sometimes white. They grow in spikes, each flower with a hood and three-lobed lower lip, the latter broad with a central notched tip, and has small purple spots, which can be seen also inside on the white of the lip. A long spur sticks out across the stem of the flower. The sepals stand upright like wings behind the hood. The bracts are purplish.

The leaves are oblong, and the upper ones sheathe the stem. They usually have conspicuous purplish black blotches on them.

The stem is solid.

Orchis: Gk. name for the plant.
Mascula: Lat., 'male.'

266

COMMON SPOTTED ORCHIS

Orchis Fuchsii

Found: Woods, damp places, fields. Common in Britain. *Flowers:* Spring and early summer. *Height:* 6 in. to 2 ft.

Before fully out the flower spike may have a rather conical appearance, a number of almost grass-like leaflets (bracts) hiding the buds or young flowers in a greenish plume. The flowers finally grow into a pale purple or lilac oblong spike, each with a broad lip dotted and streaked with purple, and cut into three lobes, the centre one a pointed V-shape.

The leaves are narrow, keeled, and taper to a point, 6–7 in. long. They are spotted with dark purple; the lower leaves are more oval and the lowest is shorter and blunter than the others. The upper leaves are silvery underneath and clasp the stem.

The stems are solid.

Orchis: Gk. name for the plant.

Fuchsii: After Leonhard Fuchs, a German botanist of the sixteenth century.

267

PYRAMIDAL ORCHIS
Orchis pyramidalis

Found: Chalky places, downs, banks, and fields. In several parts of England and Ireland in abundance, and in a few places in Scotland. *Flowers:* Summer. *Height:* 1 ft. or more.

The shape of the attractive head is distinctly like a pyramid before all the flowers open, later it becomes rather more oblong. The spike can be as long as three or even four inches, the lower lip of each flower is broad and cut into oblong lobes, the upper lip is like a hood, and the spur is rather long and slender. There are long purple bracts below each flower.

The leaves are narrow, lance-shaped, and pointed. They are not spotted, the upper leaves clasp the stem entirely.

The stem is slender and upright.

Orchis: Gk. name for the plant.
Pyramidalis: Lat., 'like a pyramid.'

BEE ORCHIS
Ophrys apifera

Found: Chalky districts, dry fields. In eastern
and southern counties of England. In middle
and south of Ireland. Not in Scotland.
Flowers: Early summer. *Height:* 4–18 in.

The flowers grow well apart at the head
of the stem in a loose spike, two to six
only. Each flower has a long green bract
below it. The three sepals are oval,
spreading and wing-like, and have a green
line down the centre of each. The petals
are small and stand up straight and are
downy. The central lip is rounded, broad,
and furry like a bee's body, velvety brown
with gold showing through.

The leaves are pale green and very narrow,
they clasp the upper part of the stem. The
lower leaves more lance-shaped.

The stem is often only 5–6 in. tall.

Ophrys: From Gk. *ophrus*, 'eyebrow,' from
the markings on the tip of the flower.

Apifera: From Lat. *apis*, 'bee,' and *ferre*, 'to
bear,' i.e. bee-bearing.

FRITILLARY
Fritillaria Meleagris

Found: Damp fields and meadows. Rather rare. Truly wild only in southern and eastern England, but not in Scotland or Ireland. *Flowers:* Spring. *Height:* 12–18 in.

A delicate and lovely bell-shaped flower, distinctively chequered or mottled with dull red, which droops singly at the head of the stem. The flower head is made up of six 'floral leaves,' which are oblong or narrowly oval, narrowing to a point, and about 1½ in. long. The colour varies from deep maroon red to a paler shade, and may even be white (p. 54) or yellowish. The flower opens out into a wide bell with bright yellow stamens in the centre.

The leaves are grass-like, 6–8 in. long, and grow from the stem. The stem is slender and upright, leafy, with a slightly reddish tinge.

Fritillaria: From Lat. *fritillus*, 'a dice-box,' in allusion to the chequered markings on the flower, like the board on which dice were thrown.

Meleagris: Gk., 'guinea-fowl,' referring to the markings of the flower, like that bird's feathers.

270

INDEX

271